Tying the Knot

THE FAITH AND BUSINESS MINISTRY

The Faith and Business Ministry serves as a much-needed tie between business and ministry to equip women, and the men who serve with them, to operate in kingdom principles. We create a pathway to share wisdom and encouragement through skill-based trainings, networking, social media, seminars, and our annual conference.

Connect with Debora D. Taylor for your next event:
Website: *www.DeboraDTaylor.com*
Facebook: *Faith and Business:*
    Tying the Knot Between Ministry and the Marketplace
Email: *DeboraDTaylor@DeboraDTaylor.com*
Phone: 888.584.9058

Taylor-Made International
P.O. Box 1554
Collierville, TN 38027

Available Services
    Motivational Speaking and Teaching
    Business Coaching
    Leadership Training
    Executive and Group Travel Consulting
    Spiritual / Life Coaching

Tying the Knot
BETWEEN MINISTRY AND THE MARKETPLACE

Mastering the Mountains
Through Our Spiritual Influence

DEBORA D. TAYLOR, FOUNDER

Cover Design and Layout:
Brennan Hill * Bhill Arts & Graphics * *BHillArts@gmail.com*

Project Management / Interior Design and Layout:
Dell Self * Speak Through Me Publishing * *www.STMPub.net*

In memory of Avis Nichols, my dear friend
and co-author in volume 1 of *The Faith and Business Series*

CONTENTS

Foreword 9

Acknowledgments 11

Introduction 13

Family 15

    The Cornerstone of a Family: Jennifer A. Marion 17

    Do You Want Your Family to Be Well?: ....

        Katrina McKinney Kimble 25

    Without Vision: The Marriage Will Perish: ....

        Ricky and Sheila Floyd 33

    Transforming Family Function: Beryl J. Armstrong 41

    Blending Family Cords: Patricia Hilliard 49

Religion 59

    The Media and Ministry: Belkis Clarke-Mitcham 61

    The Right to Choose: Christine A. Hinton 71

Education 77

    Wordly Wisdom and Media Influence: Anita D. King 79

    Ministry Beyond the Four Walls: Ashlei N. Evans 87

    Qualified for the Purpose: Laneice McGee 95

    From Educator to Entrepreneur: Beverly Walthour 103

Media 111

    The Power of Media Will Let Your Light Shine: ....

        Onika Shirley 113

    Don't Bring Me No Bad News: Leslie M. Dillard 121

Arts and Entertainment 129

How Many Ways Can I Give Praise?: ....

Wesliane Marie Kidd 131

#SocialSuicide: Tanya E. Lawrence.............................137

Business 147

Stepping and Standing in the Name of ....

Kingdom Business: Tina L. Byrd 149

Becoming Financially Aware: Malwante R. Stewart 157

Legacy—Encourage Diligence: Kathy L. Rivers 165

Money Management: The Key to Having a Better ....

Relationship with Your Money: Sarita Price 173

Government 185

Pursuing a Sound Mind: Katherine LaVerne Brown...... 187

Lead and Live Your Legacy: Leigh K. Ware....................197

Man's Government, God's Justice: ....

Restoration of Hope in a Lost and Broken World: ....

Staci L. Kitchen 207

Afterword...217

Meet Debora D. Taylor 219

FOREWORD

It was with great pleasure that I accepted writing the foreword to this powerful book written by my spiritual daughter, Pastor Debora Taylor, on the subject of the seven mountains. Many have not heard or understood this biblical mandate because God has certain seasons where he releases certain revelations. One of the key scriptures I teach about on these seven mountains, kingdoms or spheres, comes from Revelation 11:15 (NKJV) which states, "The kingdoms of this world have become *the kingdoms* of our Lord and of His Christ...").

So what are these kingdoms? Pastor Taylor teaches and releases the revelation on not only what they are and where they are, but also why we must take them for the kingdom and the King.

The authors in this book have shared their insight into these seven mountains, i.e., family, religion, education, media, arts and entertainment, business, and government.

We have all been called to marketplace ministry, to take the kingdom to the whole world and bring about societal change. I highly endorse this book as I know it will be a blessing to you and to the kingdom.

Apostle H. Daniel Wilson
Valley Kingdom Ministries International

ACKNOWLEDGMENTS

I want to say thank you to my husband, Guy, for his love, support, and patience. I couldn't have done it without you, Babe. Thank you for standing by my side.

My daughter, Nyshi, for inspiring and encouraging me to go forth with this book project. I love you more than words can express.

My Mom, Minnie Peller, you're the best! Thank you for having my back.

I offer heartfelt gratitude to the co-authors for their support in compiling our second anthology. Every idea in this book bears each author's fingerprint—an original identity the Lord gave every single one of them.

To my book project manager, Dell Self (Speak Through Me Publishing), for her tireless collection of data organization and implementation that gave birth to this publication.

Thank you to Brennan Hill (Bhill Arts & Graphics) for an awesome book cover design and promotional materials.

Thank you to Apostle H. Daniel Wilson for taking time out of your schedule to reach out and support me. I do not take your kindness lightly.

To my pastors, Apostle Ricky Floyd and Pastor Sheila Floyd, I am so grateful to you. You have been marvelous supporters of this project from day one. I am blessed to know you.

Finally, to my priceless son, Dominique Lamar (Lauren Powell), and to my two granddaughters, My'Asha and Gracelyn, indeed you are my generational legacy.

INTRODUCTION

An Ordinary Day

It started as an ordinary day in 1975 when two God-fearing men reunited through an unexpected opportunity of fellowship. They immediately began to discuss what God had placed on their hearts. As they shared their insights, it was clear that these two men, Dr. Bill Bright and Loren Cunningham had heard from the throne of God. Although the concept was revealed to each man separately, they were very much together in what God had said.

This meeting on what seemed like an ordinary day was the start of a movement known as the Seven Mountains. We continue to thank these men and others for their obedience in leading the way and sharing their vision for the world with the world.

Divided into seven sections, one for each mountain, this inspiring educational book addresses various aspects of each mountain from a unique perspective. Each author shares from their own experience with the intent of educating the reader on ways to stand on their mountain of influence and keep the knot tied between ministry and the marketplace.

The Seven Mountains

Family

Religion

Education

Media

Arts and Entertainment

Business

Government

Family

Family is the first and longest section in this book. It is such by design. Family was the first institution God ordained. Family is foundational and affects every aspect of life. What happens within the family network spills over to the marketplace, church, school, all types of communications, arts and entertainment, economics, and even government. What we learn at home, whether good or bad, shows up in every mountain we approach.

Gain insight from the following authors:

Jennifer A. Marion 17

Katrina McKinney Kimble 25

Ricky and Sheila Floyd 33

Beryl J. Armstrong 41

Patricia Hilliard 49

THE CORNERSTONE OF A FAMILY

Jennifer A. Marion

Satan is strategic in his attempts to attack the family unit. He attacks where there is a broken connection. Jesus Christ must be the cornerstone of a family's foundation to invade the enemy's camp and dethrone him from the mountain of family. Jesus Christ eliminates Satan's advances of breaking through and wreaking havoc in a family.

About this Author

Jennifer A. Marion

A wife, mother of six, and retired from the United States Army, Jennifer A. Marion decided to pursue her dreams of working with families. With a Master of Arts in Marriage and Family Therapy from Liberty University, her dream has come true as she works with a foster care organization that specializes in preserving families through education and skill building.

Jennifer is the founder of Empowering Visions, LLC, a life coaching practice designed to help others develop a strong sense of self, create and maintain a balanced lifestyle, and provide education to marriages and families. Jennifer is regarded as a visionary leader, yet deeply spiritual as she communicates the will of God through personal experiences and prophetic ministry.

Connect with this author and speaker for your next event:
Website: *www.EmpoweringVisions05.com/*
Facebook: *www.Facebook.com/MZ.JennMarion*
Email: *EmpoweringVisions05@gmail.com*

More from Jennifer A. Marion
  Graced for This
  Empowering Visions
  40 Days of Empowerment (forthcoming)

Available Services
  Vision Board Empowerment Workshops
  Motivational Speaking
  Women's Conferences

THE CORNERSTONE OF A FAMILY

Jennifer A. Marion

Together, we are his house, built on the foundation of the apostles and the prophets. And the cornerstone is Christ Jesus himself. We are carefully joined together in him, becoming a holy temple for the Lord.

—Ephesians 2:20–21 NLT

I grew up in a broken home where my mother provided for seven children. Children raised in broken homes can be affected in their development and behavior. I didn't have to suffer from my parent's divorce. Unfortunately, there are others who are plagued with deficiencies in more lasting issues such as mental health, developmental progress, social skills, and behavioral matters. When a home is broken, the family unit is affected. Broken families and single parents have the tendency to create conflict and chaos in a family. I have been both a single parent and a mother of a broken home. My two children suffered because they blamed themselves for the break up. They started having emotional problems, and feelings of rejection that caused them to rebel. I was neglectful of the importance of the mountain of family, but God would provide an understanding.

The mountain of family is arguably one of the most important mountains. God's love for the family unit is seen throughout the Word of God. Anything that's valuable to God, is a threat to Satan. We live in a world today where a dysfunctional family is accepted as the norm. The family is the building block of a society, and a community is dependent upon the stability of a family. A dysfunctional family produces a dysfunctional community. When a family is unsuccessful, the church, community, and nation will fail.

A marriage is significant because it is a covenant between a man and a woman that is shared with God. It's the beginning phase of a family unit and a believer's first ministry. Far too many people would rather build their family upon a broken foundation than submit to God's ways. It has become common for men to run from their responsibilities of being fathers, leaving the women to operate in both the father and mother role. Regardless of whether the man ran out or was pushed out, his absence causes everything to be out of order. Satan infiltrates a family unit by attacking the head of the household first. The absence of fathers has negatively affected this nation. The nation is experiencing a fatherless crisis, which has caused millions of children to live in a home without a biological father. This is not to say that a single parent cannot have a godly home and live blessed. However, this is not God's intended plan for his children.

Nearly every societal problem the nation is faced with today is due to a father factor. The most recurring problem with the family is the man being out of position. Satan has been successful by taking men out of the home. Because positioning in a family unit is important, when the head of the household is out of position, Satan stays atop of the mountain of family. The order of a family is Jesus, the husband, the wife, and then the children. God has a specific purpose for a family, "be fruitful, and multiply, and replenish the earth, and subdue it" (Genesis 1:28). The children of God were given dominion over the earth. Satan doesn't want us to become "kings and priests that reign on the earth." He wants to destroy the concept of marriage and the ability for a woman to bear children. Satan knows a family that functions in the fullness of God operates through the power of love. The love is first shared with the husband and wife through marriage, and then amongst the children. Satan wants to destroy this loving relationship. A powerful family in God is a threat to Satan.

Mountain of Family

Deuteronomy 7 explains how the Jebusite nation controls the mountain of family. The meaning of Jebusite is "a place trodden down." The people affected are oppressed, treated unfairly, or harshly. The Jebusites were wicked people who participated in pagan worship through abominable practices. The demons of rejection are at the entrance of the mountain of family. When someone is trodden upon or thrown away, the spirit of rejection begins to manifest. The individual thinks they are useless, vile, cast off, unaccepted, unloved, unworthy, unimportant, or simply don't belong. These are the lies of deceit the enemy whispers in their ears. Baal is the principality atop the mountain. It's through the worship of Baal the enemy seduces the nation. Satan's goal is to weaken the family one by one. People are seduced by Baal through sexual immorality, sexual perversion, devaluing of human life and relationships, compromising, and self-centeredness. 2 Timothy chapter 3 describes the perilous times that will come. Today, Satan has been successful in his attack against the family with the absence of fathers, homosexuality, cohabitations, and abortions. People have started accepting these abnormalities as normal. Making matters worse is that the government continues to implement laws which disintegrate the family unit.

Invading the Mountain of Family

There are online marketplaces where different people sell a particular good or service to others. These websites have advanced this arena tremendously—millions of people have been affected. If the world can so boldly move their agendas forward, why can't we advance the kingdom of God? God has given us abilities to be effective for the kingdom. He has given everyone the ability to influence others by operating in different areas of assignment. My life, business, and ministry represent the kingdom of God. I have a business and a job which is used to minister Christ to others. I use my sphere of influence to preserve, restore, and rebuild marriages and families. I perform these actions by counseling, coaching, empowering, inspiring, skill-building, writing, and teaching the principles of God. I'm a change agent as a marketplace leader.

There are many ways to share the message of Christ, but you have to operate in your sphere of influence. God has strategically put leaders in places of influence that will affect the mountain of family. These marketplace leaders must reclaim their mountain of influence to annihilate the enemy. It's time for believers to start using their gifts and talents given by God. To invade the mountain of family, you must first be carrying the DNA of the family of heaven. An individual must be born again in Jesus Christ and adopted into the family of God. The Holy Spirit becomes the individual's spiritual guide. We are to be led by God to fortify the family. Strengthening a family can occur by restoring, rebuilding, and recovering the family unit. My marriage and family has been successful because our foundation was built upon Jesus Christ. There have been ups and downs. No, not every day was perfect, but we knew we had to roll up our sleeves and fight for what we wanted.

The husband and wife must make Jesus Christ the cornerstone of the family. The cornerstone is a foundational stone that's used when constructing buildings or structures. The cornerstone can be seen on the outside corner of a structural building with an inscription of the construction date, name of architect or builder, or other significant individuals. However, the real cornerstone is under the building structure holding the foundation together. The other stones for that project cannot be built until the cornerstone is in place. The entire structure of a building is determined based on the cornerstone. The building could be a beautiful structure that is pleasing to the eye, but if the foundation is not good, it is worthless. A foundation that does not rot, crack, and can't be easily affected by a natural disaster is a desirable one.

The Apostle Paul referred to the "head of the corner" and "Chief Cornerstone of the Church" as Jesus Christ. We are living temples in the marketplace for God. Jesus is the only foundation that will keep our homes from collapsing. Any family that places Christ at the center will prosper. Jesus wants to be Lord in our life. His presence in the home will provide the family with happiness, satisfaction, love, respect, peace, and purpose. A family with a purpose and a mission is unstoppable. Surrender your family unto the Lord, so he can transform the home. Become a family of light in this dark world. Believers in Jesus Christ can hold to the fact that, "And it shall come to pass in the last days, that the mountain of the Lord's house shall be established in the top of the mountains, and shall be exalted above the hills; and all nations shall flow unto it" (Isaiah 2:2 KJV).

In the meantime, prayer is affective in overcoming the stronghold of Baal. Marketplace leaders must seek God to place them in positions of authority to make changes in the government. Through prayer, God is given permission on earth to release his power against the enemy. Through prayer, we can approach and fight the spirit of rejection with the love of Christ. Love conquers all. The spirit of rejection is one that likes to whisper in the ears of God's people and tell them lies. Some lies that exist are "you are worthless," "you are not accepted," "no one likes you," and "you do not deserve God's attention." Don't allow the Devil to kill your purpose, steal your joy, and destroy your family. Love is a potent weapon against the power of darkness. Stand firm in your faith and the Word of God to reclaim the mountain of family.

Mastering the Mountain

- Satan desires to create a dysfunctional family unit. He wants the family to be stricken with conflict, misbehavior, neglect, abuse, and tension. Ask God to release a supernatural power to heal, deliver, and restore your family.
- A cornerstone built in Jesus Christ is not faulty. It will hold a family together with God's love. Allow the inscription on your vessel to represent that of Jesus Christ.
- Seek God to determine your sphere of influence. Use your life, business, and ministry to share the Gospel to others. Marketplace leaders, it's time to reclaim your mountain!

Do You Want Your Family to be Well?

Katrina McKinney Kimble

Most families are surviving rather than thriving. Many families have overextended schedules that leave everyone exhausted and fatigued. Parents and children are battling each other. Each family is as unique as a fingerprint. God chose you to be a part of your family.

Though the future may look grim, there is hope. There are some families that are stable and flourishing, but the unfortunate reality is that most are not. Don't give up. Don't lose hope. Your family can be healthy and whole.

ABOUT THIS AUTHOR

Katrina McKinney Kimble

With a servant-heart, Katrina Kimble shows her passion for the connection between faith, health, and wellness through her service as a Community Health Advocate. Over the past 15 years, Katrina has educated the community about whole-person wellness through training and presentations at conventions, various congregations, and community agencies.

Armed with a bachelor degree in Human Resources Management and Leadership, Katrina has also completed The Foundations of Faith Community Nursing course at Union University and received the Health Ministry Certificate. Katrina received the Volunteer STAR Award from the Tennessee Cancer Coalition and completed the Living Compass Faith and Wellness Training to obtain a Community Wellness Advocate Certification.

Connect with this author and speaker for your next event:
Website: *www.AwakenWellnessConsulting.com*
Facebook: *Facebook.com/AwakenWellnessConsulting*
Email: *Katrina@AwakenWellnessConsulting.com*

More from Katrina McKinney Kimble
    Awaken Women Wellness Circle
    Key guest (radio shows): In the Moment with Nicole Gates/
    Walking Into a New Life with Joyce Kyles

Available Services
    Motivational / inspirational speaking for trainings,
    workshops, lunch & learns, seminars, and conferences

DO YOU WANT YOUR FAMILY TO BE WELL?

Katrina McKinney Kimble

Beloved, I wish above all things that thou mayest prosper and be in health, even as thy soul prospereth.

—3 John 1:2 KJV

In this fast paced, technologically driven society, families are constantly busy. Families have overextended schedules that leave everyone exhausted and fatigued. Families rush through life, but fail to live. Unfortunately, most families are surviving not thriving. The American dream has become a nightmare. God has been replaced by smartphones and social media which has become the lifeline of the family. There is a divine connection between faith and wellness. If we want our families to be well, we have to go back to our creator, God Almighty.

Our relationship with God should be revealed in all areas of our lives, especially through the family. The Holy Bible is the instruction manual to creating wellness for your family. We have been taught that humans consist of spirt, body, and soul. Each family is as unique as a fingerprint.

The Mindset of the Family

In your relationships with one another, have the same mindset as Christ Jesus.

—Philippians 2:5 NIV

Our smartphones and other electronic devices constantly remind us of the hottest gossip, trend, or our next social commitment. Social media encourages self-promotion. What does your family promote? What is the mindset of your family? Do you strive to have the mindset of Jesus Christ in your family?

Everything starts within your mind. It is not always about good or bad choices, but about what is healthy or unhealthy for the family. As a parent, being intentional about my choices will have a positive or negative impact on my family. Your mind must be clear of fear, distractions, and negativity to create a healthy family lifestyle. The first step is to make the decision to strive to have a mindset like Christ Jesus.

Time to Reflect

Within the next 24 hours, reflect on the mindset of your family? Write out your thoughts.

The Spirit and Body of the Family

And the very God of peace sanctify you wholly; and I pray God your whole spirit and soul and body be preserved blameless unto the coming of our Lord Jesus Christ.

—1 Thessalonians 5:23 KJV

Have you ever been driving, listening to the GPS directions and suddenly realize that you are not going in the right direction? You observe your surroundings and nothing looks familiar. You say to yourself, "How did this happen? How did I get here?" This very same scenario happens every day to families. People realize that they are sharing their home with strangers and the only thing they have in common are their last names. When the family is spiritually, mentally, and physically tired, Satan launches his heaviest attacks on the family.

There is a saying, "What you feed will grow!" What are you feeding your family's spirit and body? Do you allow them to dine on junk food, junk TV, and have limited movement during the week? Yet, you expect your family to put on their best "Holy Ghost" smile and transform into spiritual acrobats on Sunday morning. Just because society took prayer out of the schools, this is not an excuse for families to remove God from the home.

Furthermore, families must bring prayer back into the home. You may want to schedule activities outside the home, such as taking a prayer walk through the neighborhood or serve food at a homeless shelter. Stimulate the body and engage the spirit.

Time to Reflect

Review your family's activities for the last 30 days. Did these choices bring your family closer to God or each other?

The Soul of the Family

And the Lord God formed man of the dust of the ground, and breathed into his nostrils the breath of life; and man became a living soul.

—Genesis 2:7 KJV

Man did not become a living soul until God breathed into him. Stop for a moment and take a deep breathe. God created each person with a living soul. Do you need God to breathe life into your family? The soul of the family has been torn and battered by the challenges of life. If we are intentional with our time and energy, we can restore the soul of the family.

So often, we focus on what is convenient. God is calling men and women to a rescue mission to save the family. Our children are being wrecked because they do not feel loved and supported at home. With God, we can create the home environment that revives the soul of the family. Lastly, we may have to say no to a good opportunity in order to be prepared when a great opportunity becomes available for the family. We must be willing to make a short-term sacrifice for the long-term goal.

Time to Reflect

Describe the heart and soul of your family. What would you want for your family? What will be your family's legacy?

God is calling the family back to him. The mindset, spirit, body, and soul of the family can be healthy. It will require being prayerful, making intentional choices, reflecting on the results of our choices and making the necessary adjustments to ensure a better quality of health for the family.

People visit the doctor for a yearly physical or checkup. If you have transportation, you make sure your automobile has a tune-up and oil change. Why do we do this? We know that regular maintenance is required to keep our bodies and transportation functioning at peak performance. When was the last time you and your family had a check-up? God chose you to be a part of your family. It was not an accident. Take steps to bring wholeness and health to your family starting today.

Mastering the Mountain
- Make prayer a vital part of your home.
- It starts in your mind. Make the decision to have a Christ-like mindset.
- Schedule a family checkup.

WITHOUT VISION:
THE MARRIAGE WILL PERISH

Ricky and Sheila Floyd

Family is our primary ministry and training ground. It should mirror God's relationship with his church. When marriages are healthy, they become one of God's greatest tools for evangelism in the earth. When we discover God's plan for our marriage and family, we find peace, purpose, and prosperity.

ABOUT THESE AUTHORS

Ricky and Sheila Floyd

Ricky and Sheila Floyd are the lead pastors of Pursuit of God Transformation Center, a multi-site church in Memphis, TN and Southaven, MS. They founded the School of Marriage Enhancement in addition to serving on the boards of Families Matter and Eden Estates apartments in Memphis.

Ricky's focus is faith, holiness, purpose, vision, biblical economics, and solidarity in the family, church and community. His works were featured on the Oprah Winfrey Network.

Sheila organized the Perfection Women's Ministry and conducts Reasoning Sessions for women and men trapped by depression and abuse.

They met in San Diego, CA, reside in Memphis, TN, and are the parents of Brennan (Brittany and Brynlee) Hill, Christina (Amira) Floyd, and Ricky D. Floyd, II.

Connect with these authors and speakers for your next event:
Website: *www.RickyandSheilaFloyd.com*
Facebook: *Ricky Floyd*
Email: *Info@ThePursuitOfGod.org*

More from Ricky and Sheila Floyd
   The Husband Institute, Inc. (boys mentoring)

Available Services
   Inspirational/Motivational Speaking, Marriage Coaching, Church Trainer, and Goals Workshop

WITHOUT VISION:
THE MARRIAGE WILL PERISH

Ricky and Sheila Floyd

Where there is no vision, the people perish: but he that keepeth the law, happy is he.

—Proverbs 29:18 KJV

Our marriage is wonderful now, but it wasn't always. During the first seven years, we had no real idea of what we were doing. We experienced moments of infatuation, but many moments were miserable. In fact, we had no real knowledge of what marriage was supposed to be. Neither of us had ever seen a God-centered marriage. We were saved, raising our children and serving in church, but had no understanding of why God allowed us to meet and marry. The only bit of wisdom we had concerning marriage was the declaration we made over our lives that divorce was not an option. So, we didn't divorce and continued making each other unhappy. Finally, we concluded that if divorce was not an option, and we were going to stay together, then being unhappily married was also not an option.

We can only imagine how many couples are currently living in the same miserable state we were living in. In those early years, marital purpose was not known, therefore abuse, disorder and dishonor prevailed in our relationship. We began our marriage with no real counsel, and fear was a dominating factor. It wasn't until we discovered a vision for our marriage that our marriage began to flourish. Before that discovery, our marriage was perishing.

Discover Your Marital Vision

A vision for your marriage is when a marital or premarital couple takes an inward view of what their future would look like if they were both on one accord and were in the perfect will of God concerning their spiritual kingdom calling and earthly assignment from God. We ask couples to ask and answer these questions that if for 5-years they were on one accord and completely in the will of God, what would their careers look like, where would they be living, how much money would they be making, and whose lives would they be positively affecting? We tell them that as they continue to seek God and dream together, and seek wise counsel, they will eventually discover their marital vision.

Discovering the vision for our marriage did not come overnight. We discovered part of our marital vision while seeking marital healing. God impressed upon us to begin studying everything we could about marriage, then share it with others. This was the beginning of the School of Marriage Enhancement (S.O.M.E.). The Bible lets us know that what the enemy meant for evil, "... God meant it unto good, to bring to pass, as it is this day, to save much people alive" (Genesis 50:19–20 KJV). S.O.M.E. saved our marriage. We often say that we went through hell in our marriage so others wouldn't have to. We tell people that the thing that has made you miserable is the thing that could make you money. We are of the mindset that God gives provision for his vision. Likewise, God called us to start an outreach ministry that evolved into one church with three locations. Since 2004, we have shared the ups and downs of our marriage while encouraging the importance of discovering vision for every area of your lives. We now travel abroad teaching and training married couples and singles on how to have righteous relationships.

Develop Righteous Relationships

Families, who exist in the same household without a clear vision, often find themselves growing apart. Many households experience, debt, disease, disaster, and destruction because the individuals in the house are merely living for themselves and without a real, divine purpose. Some encounter a lack of communication, unresolved issues, distrust, and other tragic occurrences, producing unrighteous relationships. A clear vision for your marriage and family will help produce righteous relationships within the family. We define this relationship as one that is groomed in the right place at the right time, with the right people for the right motives.

Righteous relationships within the family prepare the way for generational blessings, according to Psalm 37:23–26, and they must be cultivated in a healthy marital environment. Please understand that possessing righteous relationships does not mean that mistakes won't be made, but it does mean that in the right environment you will be able to learn from your mistakes. If you are engaged in unrighteous relationships within your family, the only way to right this wrong is to make the decision that your family and other relationships must be governed by the Word of God and be coached by God-fearing couples who have been through tough times, having come out victoriously.

Determine to Walk in Agreement

In Genesis 1:26–28, we learned that God created "them," blessed "them," and spoke to "them." It's important to know that God's plan for the family is to fulfill their assignments in the earth, in agreement.

Agreement is necessary in seeing your marital vision come to pass. Vision can be considered the voice of God becoming visible to those called to make earth a reflection of heaven. Proverbs 29:18 (KJV) says, "Where there is no vision, the people perish: but he that keepeth the law, happy is he." However, where there are no persuaded people, walking in agreement, the vision will perish and no one will be happy.

One of the challenges that we see in marriage is that some men (or the senior visionary of the family) think they should not have to sell their spouse on the vision. They think that their spouse should automatically read and run with the vision according to Habakkuk 2:2 (KJV). Often, they are adamant about their spouse submitting to whatever they say, when submission is not the highest form of compliance, but agreement is. When the vision is not clear or unknown, it's likened unto a blind person leading the blind and both ending up in the wrong place according to Matthew 15:14 (KJV). Even the Prophet asked the question in Amos 3:3, "Can two walk together, except they be agreed?" Submitting yourselves one to another in the fear of God is required in a marriage, according to Ephesians 5:21 (KJV); it will take agreement to manifest your marital vision. Disagreement in the marriage leads to calamity and can terminate the fullness of prosperity promised to your family.

When Calamity Prevails:
   Vision remains undiscovered.
   Resolutions are deferred.
   Schemes are increased.
   Struggles are prolonged.
   Optimism decreases.
   Innovation is lessened.
   Victory is tough.
   Iniquity is inevitable.

Dedicate Yourself to Accomplishing Goals

In order for your vision to be fulfilled, you must sit down and define specific goals. You need to determine what you want, assess where you are, find out who can help you, how long it will take, and what has hindered you in the past.

We wanted a family that represented love, unity, and good success as opposed to the tragedies, disappointments, and failures we experienced. Ultimately, our goal was to teach others to represent that as well. We assessed that our marriage had been in a state of deception, destruction and disaster until we sought out our Bishop E. L. and Lady Ella Warren for mentorship, and submitted to their wisdom and strategies on how to have a happy family.

Plan a Yearly Vision Vacation

Every year we get away for several days to talk, pray, and just enjoy each other's company. We suggest you do the same to communicate about children, finances, schedules, sex, business, successes, mishaps, etc. Focus on God's purpose for your marriage and family. Do this every year to rediscover and recommit to your vision.

Write the Vision

Habakkuk 2:2 (KJV) tells us "... Write the vision, and make it plain upon tables, that he may run that readeth it." Often within the family, there is a vision giver and a vision runner. History and studies have shown us that when we both committed about 5-years to the written vision, the vision had a greater chance of coming to pass. As your marriage heals, begin to cast a vision for the entire family.

Commit to Daily Meditation

Joshua 1:8 (KJV) lets us know that we are to meditate on the written vision, day and night because circumstances and situations will occur that could get you off track. Meditating on your vision and goals will keep you focused and cause you to eventually walk in the prosperity and good success that God has promised you.

No matter what you believe God to do in your marriage, please remember to show forth love, grace, mercy, and patience consistently. Most importantly, don't just tolerate each other, but celebrate the small progressions accomplished by each other.

Mastering the Mountain

- It's important to discover who your source is—it should be God. Discover who your soulmate is and what your life's assignment is.
- Vision will heal and deliver your family from the pains of the past and lead them to a prosperous future.
- Walking in agreement will cause God to answer your prayers.

TRANSFORMING FAMILY FUNCTION

Beryl J. Armstrong

The aim of this chapter is to inspire readers to use their influence to bring change on the mountain of family. Readers will come away with an understanding of the purpose of this mountain, be able to clearly identify family dysfunction, get a clearer vision of family function, and be inspired to use their new-found insight to transform families.

ABOUT THIS AUTHOR

Beryl J. Armstrong

Beryl J. Armstrong lives in Homewood, Illinois with her husband and twin daughters. Beryl currently serves as a Behavioral Health Provider at Family Christian Health Center located in Harvey, IL. Beryl is the President and Founder of Precious Stone Ministries (PSM) and Co-founder of The Encounter Group (TEG). Beryl has traveled to empower people to become their best version of themselves. Beryl believes that the nature of a person can be shaped by immutable things, however, she believes that the nature of a person is mutable—it can be changed. This is why Beryl is known as a change agent.

Connect with this author and speaker for your next event:
LinkedIn: *LinkedIn.com/in/Beryl-Armstrong-LCPC-NCC-4b659b99/*
Facebook: *Facebook.com/Beryl.Armstrong.7*
Email: *BerylJArmstrong@yahoo.com*

More from Beryl J. Armstrong
   The Journey to Transformation Getting to The Root of It

Available Services
   Mental Health Conference Presenter
   Counseling Supervisor
   Inspirational/Motivational Speaker
   Spiritual/Business Leadership Development

Transforming Family Function

Beryl J. Armstrong

For all creation is waiting eagerly for that future day when God will reveal who his children really are.

—Rom 8:19 NLT

If we listen closely we can hear creation groaning. This deep cry is tied to longing to see the manifestation of the power of God through his children (Romans 8:19). God desires for his sons and daughters to use their authority to transform major expanses of influence and family in one of those areas.

Introduction

Families are the influential building blocks for our communities, cities, nations and ultimately for the world. However, family dysfunction has caused a rift in the fabric of humanity and has left many without a face, name, or voice. In today's society, we see and hear more about family dysfunction as opposed to family function. If we look at families today we can see dysfunction in most of them. Which prompts some questions as to what is the mountain of family? How is family dysfunction identified? What does God say about family function? What does a functional family look like? How can I use my influence to transform and impact the mountain of family?

The Mountain of Family

The order of family has been perverted due to situations such as children being conceived and born out of wedlock, fatherlessness, and homosexuality—to name a few. Many families of today do not depict the values and love that God intended. God promised, in his Word, that there will be a turning of the hearts of the father to the children and the hearts of the children will turn to their fathers. What is the mountain of family? This mountain represents all things that influence families, and this speaks of the ecosystem of a family unit. This ecosystem includes key players such as lawmakers, laws and policies, Department of Children and Family Services, hospitals and medical centers, schools and churches. God is moving in and through key people in these systems to influence the hearts of fathers and children in order to restore family order and transform family function. That is what the mountain of family is about.

Focusing on the Family

As a licensed clinical professional counselor, I am blessed with the opportunity to touch the lives of many families. One of the ways this opportunity is presented is when a parent brings a child in for assessment, diagnosis, and therapy to help with behavioral challenges. In the course of assessment, information is revealed that points to the child manifesting behavior that speaks to the chaos within the family unit. In these instances the patient (the child) is known as the identified patient. Identified patient is a clinical term used to describe a person that unconsciously manifests the dysfunction within the family unit. In counseling, family dysfunction is when a family is in conflict and turmoil to the point that parents are not able to properly love, care, and nurture their children. This leads to neglect, abuse, and misuse. This malfunction often causes the children to compensate or look to other means to get their basic needs for love, belonging, and esteem met. Many families do not function as God intended and as a result, we see the manifestation of dysfunction through the life of the children. Many of these children struggle with disobedience, mental illness, dishonoring parents, self-harming behavior, addictive behavior, promiscuity, and identity issues. These children are lost. While often the focus is on treating the child, the focus should be on treating the family unit.

Family Function God's Way

Let's get a general understanding of the meaning of family. Family is best described as a group of people who have a shared history and future. Family is an interesting word that can mean a lot or very little depending on one's family experience. Family can give one a sense of identity. Family can cause one to feel connected and included. On the other hand, families can negatively impact individuals and cause them to question their identity and feel rejected. Family reaches beyond the who's-related-to-who issue; it takes into account the entire spiritual, mental, emotional, and behavioral system from generation to generation.

The role of the father is so important in the family. He sets the behavioral standard within the home. God, our heavenly father, is compassionate, does not hold grudges, does not deal with us in anger, and he makes a way to atone for our wrong. Jesus, God's son, simply put, only does what he sees modeled before him. He can only do what he sees his father do. He can only say what he hears his father say. This is what is called "learned behavior" in the counseling field.

Ask yourself what behavior have you learned from your father?

A functional family is one in which there are healthy boundaries and mutual respect. A functional family is where safety abounds and feelings and opinions can be expressed without fear of rejection or judgment. Love abounds with a strong sense of connectedness. The family unit is close-knit where time is willingly spent as husband and wife, siblings, and as family. A functional family demonstrates that it is more important to connect to one another than to the digital world. Leadership is based upon teamwork and not a dictatorship. Rules are amenable and allows for teachable moments. There is mutual submission to each other and surrender to God. The family unit demonstrates accountability, quick to forgive and repent. Disagreements are handled with care and compassion. Autonomy is encouraged and accepted. Communication is clear and consistent without deception or manipulation. A functional family is where the basic needs of all are met and all are encouraged to be true to themselves–to be authentic.

The Power to Transform

In the capacity I serve, God has instructed me to do the following in order to help transform families: pray, assess, educate, motivate, facilitate, and intercede. Pray and ask for guidance and insight. Ask God to reveal the root cause of the dysfunction–areas that need to be healed. Assess the nature of the problem, the severity of the impact, level of awareness, level of functionality, level of motivation, and level of accountability. Educate the family. This creates an opportunity for them to get a greater vision for family functioning. Facilitate change by helping them to become more aware of current beliefs, rules and assumptions about family function and the behavior that continues to reinforce it. Finally intercede, stand in the gap, so that their eyes will be opened to a more excellent way of functioning. Intercession serves as a way for them to experience the transforming power and love of God through you.

Realizing where God has placed you, accepting the assignment to be an agent of change for families, and tapping into the grace bestowed upon you to influence that change. Take a moment and think about where God has placed you. Are you in a position where you can be used to influence change in family function? Yes, most of us are to some degree, because we have been birthed into a biological and spiritual family. What things can you do to facilitate change in your home, on your job, in the grocery store, etc.? There are systems that we all come in contact with daily that can be used to transform family function. Ask God to open your eyes to see how you can affect change for families. You may not serve in the capacity of a counselor, but we all can pray. Start by praying for your family, the families on your block, families in your community, families in your city, families in your state, and families in your country.

Mastering the Mountain
- A healthy family is paramount to one's overall mental, emotional, physical, and social health.
- A loving connection between husband and wife and parent and child has healing power.
- Every family member has the power to impact others in their sphere of influence.

47

BLENDING FAMILY CORDS

Patricia Hilliard

My definition of blending family cords—the intertwining of different personalities of individuals meshed as a family that are branched out either from bloodlines, adoption, re-marriage, or some other source. Each cord symbolizes individuals that have assigned plans from God. In a family, the cords can be blended together to create a unity of one strong, unbreakable cord.

The Bible says, "It is good for God's people to live in unity" (Psalm 133:10). In this chapter I will offer a glimpse of what can happen when blending family cords is intentional. The blending then prepares an individual to be equipped to be used in ministry and the marketplace.

About this Author

Patricia Hilliard

Patricia Hilliard's ministry is best described in two words: captivating and anointed. Patricia has served as a licensed minister for the past two decades. Ordained as an evangelist, she serves as an assistant pastor alongside her husband Elder James Hilliard at Vessels of Honour Church under the leadership of Apostle Bill and Dr. Brenda Bowers.

Patricia takes ministry seriously—armed with a master's degree in biblical studies, she labors in her own outreach ministry, Hands of Faith Ministry.

She is a credentialed childcare provider, and owner of Jordan Early Childhood Academy, LLC.

Connect with this author and speaker for your next event:
Website: *www.PatriciaHilliardMinistries.org*
Instagram: *@GrannyMillionaire*
Email: *EvangelistPatriciaHilliard@gmail.com*

More from Patricia Hilliard
Independent Distributor / Director—Total Life Changes
Family Blending Matters Conference 2019 (and book release) / *www.Paid2Save.com/GrannyMillionaire*

Available Services
Ministry and Motivational Speaking for Women / Workshops / Prayer Conferences / Child Care Teacher Trainings

BLENDING FAMILY CORDS

Patricia Hilliard

Behold, how good and how pleasant it is for brethren to dwell together in unity!

—Psalms 133: 1 KJV

More than ever today, it is extremely important to be able to blend family like a quilt. Each patch having different cords or threads blended together for the purpose of creating a covering of security and warmth. I often think of the quilts my grandmother, Dora, would make by hand stretched across the frame with long sticks of wood. It didn't matter that the threads, patches, and uncoordinated designs had no apparent connection. Yet, when she blended those patches all together and stuffed each patch, she ended up with an heirloom that was high quality and served a great purpose.

Taking on the adventure of blending a family can be rewarding when focusing on following the instructions of God's word. Keeping unity foremost in a family, sets the foundation of the family being a refuge for when life's challenges hit us in the face. Often, I remind myself that the Bible predicted how the times of today would be; with son against father, mother against daughter, brother and sister against one another, lack of appreciation or respect for others; with a lack of love and unity being shown. The devastation, along with endless political indifferences cannot be the focus of God's people. Our focus must stay on preparing the lives that are closest to us to be equipped to effect change in ministry and the marketplace. Our families are the training stations where we can teach with hands-on experience to move forward in life with strength. Part of our responsibility as Christians is to help one another mature.

Family Foundation

Through my continued journey in life, I have been fortunate enough to have experienced a front seat view of the logistics of blending the sometimes complicated family cords. I knew early in life that I had a passion for creating a family. I even prayed as a young girl to grow up and have two boys and two girls—my prayer was granted. I was the first born to my parents, the late William and Earlee Jordan who had been trying to have children for six years of their marriage. Imagine this, my mom was off work due to a broken leg, but when she went for a check up on the leg healing, she was informed of a new development—their first child was on the way. Me. Even better, after the delivery of their precious Patricia, one and a half months later, mom was pregnant with their second child, little sandy-haired Terri.

Momma said she was so embarrassed about being pregnant so soon after my birth. Her pastor, the late Rev. E. B. Phillips of Greater Galilee Missionary Baptist Church in Milwaukee, WI, said to her, "Girl, what's wrong with you? You're married and been trying to have children for years!" Mom said Rev. Phillips' comedic personality comforted her. The legacy of enjoying hearing family stories began there. I heard this particular story of our arrivals several times through the years of childhood. Both our parents made us the priority of their lives. They simplified what life was about in expressing love to us unconditionally. I didn't just hear Luke 6:31 "Do to others as you would have them do to you" at church; it was lived out at home. More so, it was momma that showed me how to "Blend Family Cords" by her actions giving instructions of life through her passion for parenting. She always spent time talking with us and not allowing us to believe the comparisons people made between Terri and me. She taught us that we both had gifts that would shape our futures. I had examples of blending family often from my father too, because he was the patriarch of his entire family.

I inherited a spirit of tying the knot between ministry and the marketplace from the Ware family, which was my mother's family. The Wares moved to Milwaukee from Warren, AK in 1942 and had a family restaurant. Everyone that moved here worked in there and lived with my great aunt Eddie Tinker until they got on their feet. My cousin, Beatrice Ware–Childs, opened the first black-owned motel in Milwaukee, WI. It was called The Blue Spruce. It closed in the late 90's. Many black entertainers stayed there in the 40's and 50's due to segregation in some downtown Milwaukee hotels. When my mother worked there, she was going to take linens in one of the rooms; as she walked in, there stood the great Mr. Nat King Cole. She said he was so kind and gracious. My mother's family combined ministry and the marketplace ever since I can remember. The foundation for blending family starts early and creates individuals whose gifts cause legacy in generations to come. God's people are entrusted with the treasure of the gospel and we must trust that it is the gospel that will do the work in us.

Life's Experiences and Challenges are Preparation

Indeed life is full of experiences and challenges—all here to prepare us for the greater. I've had many experiences, including dealing with a teenage pregnancy and getting married two months after high school graduation. Life was indeed giving me many lessons; but it didn't stop there. Four children and six years later, I was divorced at age twenty-five. Although I lived as a single mother for nine years, God blessed me to re-marry. I am joyful to say James Ellis Hilliard and I are in our 28th year of marriage.

Life had another lesson for me. A lesson I never envisioned having to learn. Unless it is a life-threatening illness, no parent expects to lose their child before them in death. Losing my oldest child, my 24-year-old daughter was the most horrific experience in my life. Yet, my daughter's unexpected death pulled our already close family into pillars of strength for one another. Her death affected each person differently. She left a 14-month-old toddler that I raised as my fifth child. The stories in between the above occurrences gave me opportunities to strongly grow into my callings of a wife, parent, evangelist, interceder, business owner, mentor, and coach.

In the Bible, Proverbs 22:6 (KJV) says, "Train up a child in the way he should go: and when he is old, he will not depart from it," was one of my favorite scriptures in my younger years of parenting. I hung on to it when my children were babies. It wasn't until my stair step aged children were in their teen years that the challenges became harder, and I began to question that scripture. My sons were acting like the old folks would say, "They act like they ain't had no home training!" My oldest son was living a criminal life, and his brother, my youngest child, would not leave his side. I believe, "as we teach and train our children in the word; it doesn't mean there won't be some stumbling and falling. Yet, we have to believe when we have seeded the word, it shall not return to

God void." Blending disobedient children becomes so diffi- cult and makes a parent want to give up. The power to keep going is in speaking God's word over our children no matter what we see them doing. When I was over the youth depart- ment in church as minister, and respected by so many other youths, I had to believe God's word for *my* sons. I never stopped calling them men of God. I would anoint them with oil and speak God's word over them as they slept at night. After they moved out, they never came running for me to get them out of trouble, but when I heard Patrick was going to court for breaking the law; I went to the courtroom to sit and pray during his hearings for God's perfect will. I trusted God to fulfil the manifestation of who he said they were when they were in my womb. Again, no matter what I saw, I called them men of God!

Keys to Remember:
- Believe God's Word and speak and pray over your family in every situation.
- Anoint your family with oil.
- Show your children how to receive Christ as their Savior.
- Have family meetings and Bible studies.
- Laugh and laugh a lot! Forgive and ask for forgiveness.
- Listen, listen, and listen.

Blending Results: An Unbreakable Bond

My family worked by my side in my outreach ministry, Hands of Faith Ministry in Milwaukee, WI, through my flower shops, catering, wedding planning, and child care businesses; even though they would sometimes complain as teenagers. I now see their skills and gifts being used in ministry and the marketplace.

The following are some family members' expressions of what blending family cords meant to them.

My sister, Minister Terri Jordan: "I grew up with a strong influence of family and faith since childhood. Faith was the foundation that shaped my personality, beliefs, life goals and ability to give unconditional love. Along with my faith was the feeling that I was blessed with the best parents in the world and a sister who treated me like her best friend. My family exposed me to women who were God-fearing, generous, powerful, humble, confident and brilliant leaders. The legacy of those women, especially my mother, will forever impact my life."

My daughter, Tonya Penman: Tonya is my comedic child, so she sent me this note: "Family is so important to me because it's a special, unbreakable bond created by God. No matter what choices I make whether the choices are good or bad l know that my family is going to be my support system. It's like God gave me preassigned best friends. They are my best critiques as well as the strongest shoulders to cry on. My family is extra special because of our mutual thirst for Christ. I'm assured in knowing that the family I have Bible study with and pray with now will also be with me in Paradise when I'm kicking it with Shadrach, Meshach, and Abednego."

My grandson, Taishawn Toney: "You can't live without family in my opinion. They're the people that are supposed to be there when you mess up as well as when you do great things. I remember whenever I would ride my bike in the street, I would get a stern glare from family like I wasn't supposed to be doing that at all. Now that I live in Georgia and see the difference in the street activity between here and Milwaukee, I understand the lesson that was being taught. I wouldn't know anything that I wasn't being taught at school without family."

Blending Prayer Results

Daughter, Tonya Toney-Penman is a beautiful wife to my outstanding son in law, Anthony of 12 years, and mother to Courtney and Preston, an Independent Distributor for TLC and Floral designer).

Son, Patrick Toney is now finishing his Master's Degree, Rev. Patrick Toney is in leadership at Lizzie Chapel Baptist Church, Macon, GA, married for ten years to beautiful Lea, and parents to, Taishawn (freshman in college), Venaia, and Johnathan.

Son, Richard Toney Sr. is a faithful leader at Lamb of God Baptist Church, Milwaukee, WI, as well as a leader on his job. Richard is a committed husband to beautiful Le'Che, married for eight years, and model father to Richard Jr., realtor, and Independent Distributor for TLC.

*Son, William Toney (*the fourteen-month-old toddler my oldest daughter blessed me with) is now a junior at University of Wisconsin, a leader in our church, and an Independent Distributor for Amway.

Mastering the Mountain

- Be intentional in making sure you build a strong foundation reinforced with the structure of the word of God for your family.
- Realize that each individual may need to have a custom plan for their gifts to shape the future for ministry and the marketplace.
- Blending, or training, doesn't stop because you don't see immediate results, so keep speaking life (Word of God), not death over your family.

Religion

Second only to the family, the church is one of God's greatest institutions. Jesus calls it his bride. As believers, we are the church. Whether the spiritual church or brick and mortar, the church (religion) has led the way in shaping the United States of America. We have led the way in establishing schools, hospitals, and other help organizations.

Though once a dominating force, it's high time we reclaim the mountain of religion.

Gain insight from the following authors:

Belkis Clarke-Mitcham 61

Christine A. Hinton 71

THE MEDIA AND MINISTRY

Belkis Clarke-Mitcham

In "The Media and Ministry," Belkis Clarke-Mitcham addresses the importance of foundational values and how to continuously integrate them as essential parts of who we are professionally and as individuals. She poignantly outlines how to maintain integrity and spiritual principles at work and how to develop an intimate relationship with God that transforms lives.

ABOUT THIS AUTHOR

Belkis Clarke-Mitcham

Belkis Clarke-Mitcham knows brokenness. Her story reveals chapters of abuse, incest, depression, self-hate, and suicide. Today, however, her chapters tell of courage, strength, and the unleashing of her light through a phenomenal relationship with God.

A past youth leader, journalist, and teacher who has taught at every level from pre-school to university, Belkis Clarke-Mitcham graduated top of her class with a bachelor's degree in English and also holds a master's in Human Communication. A revolutionary spiritual life coach and dynamic motivational speaker, she offers inspired support while helping persons heal and display their unique selves boldly and unapologetically.

Connect with this author and speaker for your next event:
Website: *www.BelkisClarke.com*
Facebook: *Facebook.com/BelkisClarke/*
Email: *Phenro@BelkisClarke.com*

More from Belkis Clarke–Mitcham
    Workshops: Unmasked
                   Suicide to Success
                   Unleashed

Available Services
    Motivational Speaking
    Coaching: Spiritual Life
                   Sexual Abuse Survivors

The Media and Ministry

Belkis Clarke-Mitcham

The integrity of the upright shall guide them: but the perverseness of transgressors shall destroy them.

—Proverbs 11:3 KJV

The kiss of a cool Caribbean wind, wafted through the singular door thrown open and rested gently on the sweat glistened cheeks of adults lounging on couches and chairs and then sank beneath the weight of the heat to rest on the dampened brows of children scattered among adult's feet in various positions of recline on the carpet-covered floor. All eyes were glued to the television. It was 7:00 PM, and an almost reverent silence descended as the musical introduction that signaled the start of the local news penetrated the localized heatwave in the crowded room. News, a mandatory activity in our household. No one was allowed to speak and movements were met with harsh reprimands to sit still. As kids, we learned quickly the sanctity of that half hour. To underscore the importance of the news, every Monday morning our teachers expected each student to have three news items, a local story, a regional story, and an international story. The news was not questioned, the validity of stories was not examined, the idea of intentional angling of an event was not something we were taught. And religion, religion was never mentioned in the media unless it was in the paid notices or a scandal of a significant magnitude.

Similarly, in true Caribbean fashion, attending church every week was as much a requirement as those evenings on the floor listening to the 'gospel' of the media. I was awakened earlier than my play-worn body appreciated, to have the mop of strands I carried proudly on my head twisted and tugged into some sort of order that made me smile at myself in the mirror. My siblings and I were reluctantly stuffed into our "nice clothes" and made to walk the half mile or so wrapped in the sweltering heat of the Caribbean sun with a Bible and hymnal held high in a vain attempt to shield our faces from the wrath of the sun. It was a relief to approach the house of the Lord. Not because our soul was in dire need of the refreshing touch of the Holy spirt, but because there was a public water pipe just outside the church that we gulped from, to relieve our thirst, and there was shade inside the building from the fiery beast in the sky. Yes, church attendance was not an option. However, I cannot say that I recall the church having a relationship with the media unless it was to advertise an upcoming event. Amazingly, both institutions wield significant influence yet the two are wary of each other.

Years later, the two childhood activities would form the foundation for the shaping of my life. As a Christian and a journalist, I would unintentionally become a voice for religion, the downtrodden, the broken, and the at-risk of our communities. I was no maverick, no activist. I was a young journalist who could not stand duplicity or dishonesty. I was bored by the empty rhetoric of politicians and leaders. I was dismayed that human interest was not sufficiently highlighted via mass media. My personal relationship with God made me realize that though the media did not use its vast influence to promote God and his principles, did not mean I had to follow that trend. I remembered a high school principal saying to me that in her house 7:30 PM was a date with Belkis. They eagerly awaited to hear what stories I would bring, what hope I would inspire and to see who would be featured. My relationship with God taught me that God is the ultimate voice with the most important information for humanity. He is the source of hope, inspiration, deliverance and destiny. So instead of falling in line, a young naive journalist carved a path for herself and used the media that wanted nothing to do with God because he was not sensational or tangible enough as an avenue for sharing his principles and reaching into the hearts and homes of many through everyday stories of hurt, brokenness, healing and triumph that were media acceptable. I was a very small, certainly unknown, voice in the wilderness that was the media, so I was happy to accept the small stories. The stories that I was told would never bring me fame. That was okay. I became the voice of, churches, schools, orphanages, and organizations that were seldom, if ever, considered newsworthy. I did not just share their events, I promoted their stories, principles, values and impact on our communities. Unwittingly, fame came. But for me I was humbled to be able to use this taboo medium for twelve years to consistently share the principles of God via human interest stories.

The media influences—that goes without saying. The Agenda Setting Theory is one theory that supports this. The media is a constant voice that filters across barriers to infiltrate homes and minds planting ideas that are repeated until they germinate and take root. Unfortunately, they are hardly seeds of God and his principles. Religious sects do not trust the media. They accuse the media of sensationalism that stirs the passion of the masses. On the other hand, the media does not trust churches, they see them as secretive institutions that hide facts and take advantage of the passions and needs of the masses. Two major influences, none promoting the value of the other. Scarcely ever is there a news story that expounds on the values of God and the importance of these values. The role and function of religious sect is hardly, if ever, touched on by the media. Furthermore, religious sects continue to struggle with how to develop a relationship of such magnitude that the media not only relay scandals or events, but the values and practices of the church. It seems an impossible road to navigate.

In an ideal world, the media would recognize the monumental value of religious teachings and eagerly use its influence to promote said values. But, alas, we live in a less than ideal world. Consequently, out of fear of the skepticism that is a trademark of journalism, the church hangs back, afraid its flaws would be exposed and the positives overlooked. Conversely, promoting what appears to be mundane values and traditions, and faith in an unseen God is not news worthy. The media certainly has no interest in selling viewers a story about a personal relationship with God. Not when the depravity of humanity can be explored, exploited, and sold to viewers and result in higher ratings. The scandal, horror, and insanity of humanity tells a more fascinating story than that of knowing your creator and developing a relationship with him. The media has very little interest in most cases in letting humanity know that the madness that we face daily can be combatted and that there is hope when we develop a relationship with God. Added to that we live in a world that seeks to be politically correct. Therefore, to avoid excluding one religious sect and the viewers along with it, no religious teachings are promoted by the media. Meanwhile, the church cowers in fear, hiding its flaws and ultimately also hiding its potential for impact. Therefore, one cannot look to the media for information on how to develop (or the importance of developing) a personal relationship with God.

A personal relationship with God is critical in my ministry. As a motivational speaker, (sometimes deliverer of the Word) and spiritual life coach, I teach people the art of authentic living, how to be internally healed of the many traumas we face, how to tap into their God-designed purpose and unleash the light he has given them onto the world. I remind individuals that it's ok to live fiercely, boldly, and authentically for God. I am a living witness that he still rescues; after the trauma of incest, sexual abuse, and molestation as well as physical and emotional abuse, I rose from suicide to success. I am reminded that he is a miracle worker – I have two degrees that were covered by full scholarships. I reiterate that he cares and heals; he has healed my inner self to reflect His glory outwardly. Yes, my God desires intimacy. I know what it is like to not know where I end and God begins because he draws me in that closely. A personal relationship with God is the greatest relationship one can experience. It is not about following a prescription and then saying God must do this or that. It is a desire for Him whether he does something for you or not, a desire that consumes, and knowing he desires you in like manner (Ephesians 3: 17–19).

How can you move past a passionless routine? Now this is where things become awesome. Building a relationship with God can be likened to constructing a relationship with the man or woman of your dreams.

- *Meeting*: There is the initial meeting where interest is sparked. Something about God catches your eye or stirs your curiosity and you want to know more. That develops into acquaintanceship.

- *Acquaintances*: You get to know a few details and eagerly await the next encounter. This may be the next church service, radio program, Bible study, or time you have set aside to talk (prayer). Soon that acquaintanceship develops into a friendship.

- *Friendship*: Like sincere friends, you interact often (growing prayer life). The thing about interaction with a friend is that one person does not do all the talking. It is shared talking and listening. The more you listen to the individual the more easily you recognize the voice (familiarity with God's voice develops).

- *Courtship*: As more time is spent with the person, the emotional attachment grows and both individuals desire increased time together. You do not want to miss anything from each other so you devour text messages (personal Bible reading and meditation; Joshua 1:8). You do not hesitate to answer the phone (responding to God's call). You long to hear his voice (prayer time, meditation, sensitivity to his presence). You want to know everything there is to know (you hungrily listen to sermons and teachings about God). As the friendship grows, you both express an interest in sharing a deeper connection and so the courtship ensues.

- *Marriage*: The information shared is more intimate and the time spent together gets longer. Soon a lifetime commitment is established (God reveals the secrets of his heart). A mutual love that is life-transforming blossoms. His voice becomes the most important voice and trust grows because you have seen that he is dependable, faithful, and does not deceive you.

Relationship building takes time, honesty, commitment and interest. It involves caring most about God and what pleases his heart and trusting that he cares about us and what pleases our heart. When we establish this type of relationship our faith grows. We cannot have faith in someone we do not know. You need to know God, not know about him. Just like you know your closest friend, your child or your lover. Additionally, the principles that govern your relationship do not disappear when you leave the house. So, it is with God. No matter where you are you desire to live in a manner that pleases him and preserve the integrity of your relationship with him. Therefore, if you work in the media remember, when everyone else is seeking the angle to bring fame and fudging on values and truth, make your name by pursuing truth. Seek God to show you a path of truth. When others seek to use the media only for the promotion of the most sensational story, pursue the most meaningful stories. There is an audience waiting to hear.

Reminders for Conquering this Mountain

- Be a Christian example. Do not deny your faith. It is easy to skip over your relationship with God in pursuit of being accepted by a wider audience, but everyone needs God, and needs hope (Matthew 10:33).
- Don't water down your beliefs: I know who God is and what he has done for me. He is doing it for others. As you tell their stories, you will tell others about him.
- Do not compromise on your core spiritual principles: I have had to let offers go because they undermined my beliefs, discredited God, and were counterproductive.
- Maintain your integrity; values can pull viewers. There are people in need of hope, transparency, and honesty.

- Let your angle always be a principled angle: be consistent in truth (Proverbs 12:22). Never be afraid to reflect the principles that govern your faith. Your relationship with God should not only extend to the breadth and length of the room you live in.
- God is bigger than ratings and sensationalism; pursue Him and promote Him. Your success will follow.
- You are the church: be more influential than the media. People can't ignore you when you are the most influential. Use the media as an avenue. You do not have to be a preacher. Let your stories reflect God's principles.
- God is not a religion or a system. He is the Supreme Being who requires a sincere passionate relationship with his creation. No matter your marketplace, you can live his principles, maintain a relationship with him that adds perspective, purpose, healing, and hope to your life.

Mastering the Mountain
- Building a relationship with God is like building a relationship with the man or woman of your dreams.
- Your relationship with God should not only extend to the breadth and length of the room you live in.
- No matter your marketplace, you can live God's principles, maintain your relationship with him and embrace a fascinating intimacy that adds perspective, purpose, healing and hope to your life.

THE RIGHT TO CHOOSE

Christine A. Hinton

In this chapter, I will discuss a part of my early childhood, how I dealt with childhood polio, and the effects it had on my life growing up. I will also share about some of the choices that I made and the resulting negative effects. Most importantly, I want to tell how I established my relationship with the Lord, and the transformation that took place in my life because I chose to answer God's call on my life.

ABOUT THIS AUTHOR

Christine A. Hinton

Christine A. Hinton, young at heart and full of fun resides in Wisconsin. She treasures her time with her extensive family. Christine is the second oldest of nine children, with three children of her own, eleven grandchildren, and four great-grandchildren.

As an ordained minister of the gospel and member of Abundant Faith Church of Integrity (Milwaukee, WI), Christine is devoted to preaching and teaching the message of Christ. Christine operates her own business as a travel-marketing consultant.

Connect with this author and speaker for your next event:
LinkedIn: *LinkedIn.com/in/Christine-Hinton-8036a3108*
Facebook: *Christine Auretta Hinton*
Email: *ChristineAHinton6@gmail.com*

More from Christine A. Hinton
Intercessory prayer

Available Services
Inspirational speaking and ministry
Augustine's Travel Service (owner and marketing consultant)

The Right to Choose

Christine A. Hinton

For I know the thoughts that I think toward you, says the Lord, thoughts of peace and not of evil, to give you a future and a hope.

—Jeremiah 29:11 NKJV

Growing up, I had to deal with the trauma of suffering from the effects of childhood polio. As a little girl I was treated differently by people. I came through multiple surgeries which affected my health and nearly took my life. I was delivered from many things over the course of my life which caused me to depend on the Lord. I was delivered from abuse, low self-esteem, drugs, and alcohol. I was at a low point in my life thinking to myself that there had to be more to life than just existing. I was baptized at the age of eight years old, but did not have a personal relationship with the Lord until I was forty-two years old. When I gave my life to the Lord, everything changed from bad to worse, so it seemed to me. People thought I was just going through a phase.

I was on fire for the Lord, so I went around telling anyone who would listen how the Lord turned my life around. My encounters with my family were strained, so I invited them to come to church. Twenty-one members of my family gave their lives to the Lord! The Lord, in his infinite wisdom, used me to be a light in a world of darkness. I was shunned and told that it didn't take all of that, but for me it took a lot more. I found myself seeking and chasing after the Lord because I knew my life depended on him. I knew that I had a purpose in God's plan for my life.

I never thought that my life mattered or that I had any impact on the lives of my family until we came together and talked about it. I understand that how one lives their life before others has an impact on them. I always thought that I was in control of my own life, even if it went bad I could choose my own way. I met a man named Jesus who showed me a better way to live and I knew in my heart that it was the best decision I had made.

We make choices every day to do things or not to. When dealing with life choices the one thing I know that works is seeking the Lord for the answers to life's questions. Most times, we try to do things in our own strength and when it turns out bad we get upset or want to quit trying to do better; I learned that we will make mistakes but shouldn't quit. When you put family with religion, it works out better for the individual and family as a whole. I think sometimes we are too hard on ourselves and try to live up to family legacies that are often times unrealistic. The positive effect of this is that faith in God does and can work.

Religion has had a major influence in my life to the point that I no longer make excuses for my past life choices; I no longer allow my past to dictate or influence my present or future. I was big on making excuses for why I couldn't start or finish things. I was afraid of success. I didn't think I qualified or even had a chance in being successful in life. I always thought myself as less than. How could the Lord use me for anything? I did not think I was worth it.

In ministry, I am an intercessor, teacher, and ordained minister. These things the Lord made me. I have come to understand that there is more to living for the Lord than just being happy being saved. The Lord has given us gifts, talents, and the ability to do his will in the earth. My family supported me in my decision to live this life that I chose. My relationship with some of my family is still a bit strained, but I gave it to the Lord.

I still encourage them to be the best at what their life endeavors may be, I pray for them constantly, and I strive to be all that the Lord would have me to be. I tie the knot between family and religion by being the example. There is nothing impossible or too hard that the Lord can't fix. The Lord is relational and so he made us to be relational also. I have learned that I am only one person and I can't be everything to everybody.

I used to burn myself out trying to fix everybody not realizing that I needed to be fixed. When we take a step back and regroup, pray and wait on the answer, it will be the answer that we need for the situation or circumstance we are facing; then we will be able to handle it in a better way without being stressed.

It is important to know that your strength is in the Lord. You must believe that you can do anything you set your heart and mind to do, if you will just keep him in the forefront of everything. You may have to take a stand on what you believe. Against opposition, just stand. There is always someone watching to see if you make it or break it. There is someone who needs what you have to share. Allow the Lord to lead and guide you. I drive a school bus of children who are disrespectful to authority. At first I was going to quit on the spot, but the Lord said they needed me to be their driver.

I wrestled with the decision of quitting or staying, I started out by complaining and murmuring about it and then I got mad, at myself. I took a stand and decided in my heart that I would be the light of love and kindness to these children no matter what. I pray in my bus every morning and evening; I pray over the seats the children sit in, and also pray for the children, their parents, and teachers. Now, that spirit of rebellion no longer can stay on my bus and ride. I realize the power that the Lord has given me and I use my spiritual gifts of prayer and intercession, so that my day is peaceful. The children's behavior is a work in progress. I know that it will work out for their good as I plant seeds of peace each day.

In spite of any of life's circumstances, situations or challenges you may face, remember that you have a helper who patiently waits for you to call, so keep on praying and expecting without ceasing. He will answer you. It is not about a title, how much money you have, or material wealth, it is about the peace that passes all understanding, it is about standing firm in your faith and not compromising your self-worth, you are the solution to any problems that may arise in the marketplace. Never change who you are to fit in, just be you.

As we stand on this mountain of religion, remember that everything you need in order to tie the knot between ministry and the marketplace can be found in Christ Jesus. You have the right to choose a life in Christ no matter what anyone else thinks or says.

Mastering the Mountain
- Don't count yourself out.
- Have faith even when you don't see it.
- Our ever-present Lord knows what we need.

Education

In the Bible, God was constantly telling his people to teach his laws to their children. He wanted his commandments recited daily for everyone to know.

The original purpose of formal education in the United States was to train people to read and share the Bible. Almost all of the Ivy League schools, such as Harvard, Yale, and many more, were started to train people in some form of ministry. Things are very different from that now. It's time to reclaim this mountain through our Christian influence.

Gain insight from the following authors:

Anita D. King 79

Ashlei N. Evans 87

Laneice McGee 95

Beverly Walthour 103

WORDLY WISDOM AND MEDIA INFLUENCE

Anita D. King

God entrusted me with the gift of teaching which led to a twenty-five year career as a master educator for children and adults in schools and other venues. Standing on the mountain of education with its revolving doors is stunning. Climbing is challenging, while sustaining the knowledge breeds wisdom. Media types allow human interaction instantly. A marriage of education and media opens portals of power and progress waiting to be used. So, gear up and stand with me. Let us discover how to use our knowledge, Bible, gifts, faith, and technology to reach the world through media in a positive way.

ABOUT THIS AUTHOR

Anita D. King

Educated, gifted, and passionate are just a few ways to describe Anita D. King—a manifold woman of God. With a Master of Education degree, Anita has been blessed to teach, supervise, and develop ministries.

Anita shows her gifts through her writing and speaking. Previously, she was in banking and sales. Although Anita is an early retiree pursuing her fourth career, in addition to exploring homemade natural products, her heart has remained steadfast in caring for her family. With so much on one plate, Anita still finds time to have fun—she loves a good road trip.

Connect with this author and speaker for your next event:
Website: *www.AnitaDKings.com*
Twitter: *@PPrayerCloset (Personal Prayer Closet)*
Email: *Info@AnitaDKings.com*

More from Anita D. King
  God Reminders
  Signature Healing Series (best-selling inspirational audio)

Available Services
  Event speaker
  Ministry through inspirational audio narratives

Wordly Wisdom and Media Influence

Anita D. King

All Scripture is inspired by God and is useful to teach us what is true and to make us realize what is wrong in our lives. It corrects us when we are wrong and teaches us to do what is right. God uses it to prepare and equip his people to do every good work.

—2 Timothy 3:16–17 NLT

God entrusted me with the gift of teaching which led to a twenty-five year career as a master educator for children and adults in schools and other venues. However, it didn't start out that way.

Meager Beginnings

I received a phone call from my friend Cathey one night. She was on a prayer mission because the health of her close friend, Denise, was declining from cancer. She asked if I could create something she could share with her friend to promote hope and encouragement. Hanging up the phone, I went into prayer for direction. Later, as I was carefully researching and reading every scripture in the Bible on healing I could think of, God took over. I began reading, "And, behold, a woman, which was diseased with an issue of blood twelve years, came behind him, and touched the hem of his garment: For she said within herself, If I may but touch his garment, I shall be whole" (Matthew 9:20–21 KJV).

It was then God spoke to me. It was clear I had to use this remarkable story of healing as a key to Denise's own healing. He charged me with creating something that would eventually benefit everyone. God began to steer me toward amazing tools of technology that served his purpose. I completed the project, sent it to Cathey, and started on the next message. Meanwhile, Cathey delivered the CD to Denise, who was so inspired and encouraged she listened to it around the clock. Imagine that for a moment. God's words, and my voice making such a difference. The audio message of *The Hem* was so powerful for Denise that within days, her faith began to strengthen. Her body got stronger. Her hope was renewed. Her relationship with God got even stronger. Within six months, her cancer was dissipating and today she is cancer free. Praise God!

One phone call, prayer, and God's guidance changed my life and ministry. I am now reaching the world and changing lives by educating with media. Are you equipped for God to do the same for you? The answer is yes. You hold all the necessary gifts, tools, and qualifications to open your ministry to the world. I pray this chapter will help you change lives by:

- tapping into your "wordly" wisdom (the wisdom from your words),
- becoming proficient in technology,
- setting the standard for excellence when spreading the Word of God.

Words, Words, Words

Your wordly wisdom can change your world. The mountain of education shelters our knowledge base. It is up to us to use what we know to impact people in all walks of life. For instance, it is much easier to smile than frown, or say kind words as opposed to unkind words. Go ahead, try it. When people hear words they also hear the emotion behind them. Let's face it, we are not always wise in the things we say. We are equipped with so many beautiful things to say. Imagine how your ministry could increase by choosing wise words. Words that change, impact, encourage, liven, etc., are powerful to you and your anointing. It is my experience that carefully thought out words along with compassion yield beneficial results. If you are reading this book, you are educated in words. Education does not stop after the degree. We learn new things daily. So, take larger steps by adding to your vocabulary to further empower your messages. Connecting to people using words is powerful. I encourage all to research new words that will bring color and character to your messages. Use words to point to the Savior and his love—not words to bring attention to a large vocabulary.

> *Reminder*: When she speaks, her words are wise, and she gives instructions with kindness (Proverbs 31:26 NLT).

Technology: From Woeful to Successful

"But Mrs. King, I am not computer savvy!" You cannot imagine how often I heard those words while training adults. The funny thing is many *are* savvy, but their fear blocks progress. As you know, words are important to the survival of ministries. Believe me, using your words with today's technology will usher you to another level. Like you, I am encouraged and given many compliments on my messages and their delivery. I never imagined that my voice, my words, and a computer would change Denise's life.

Always a fan of technology, I embraced it head on and it has served me well. It can do the same for you. Tying the knot between ministry and the marketplace may involve heavy use of technology and media which could have a significant impact on this mountain when used with our gifts and words. That is why we love what we see and hear. It is proven that visuals, audios, dynamic effects and other tools, make wonderful learning platforms. Look forward to your social influence solidifying Christian faith.

> *Reminder*: "Keep putting into practice all you learned and received from me—everything you heard from me and saw me doing. Then the God of peace will be with you" (Philippians 4:9 NLT).

Education, Media, and Ministry—Tools for Living

A few years ago, I was reading the article "Should Christians Sell, Market, and Promote Products and Services?" by Frank Viola. At that time, I was struggling with pricing my products and services. Don't get me wrong, I still struggle sometimes, but I understand better how God views my income and contributions. The article exposed viewpoints from readers about whether ministries should profit from sharing God's Word. I found out this viewpoint is called "selling Jesus," which I feel is designed to promote guilt. This argument will go on until the end of time, but I learned from that article, and other articles, that God has gifted us with the tools we need to survive. God is interested in our prosperity and being able to provide for our families and ourselves. I have also learned that God equipped women and men to sell their goods to make money.

Combining media and education produces ministry for many. This is an extraordinary addition to the mountain of education.

Education is important to God. Honestly, everything holds educational value. God spent time in earlier days educating his children on how to live. He supervised Adam as he named every animal, plant, and species in earth in Genesis 2:19–20. He taught Noah how to build the ark in Genesis 14–16. He tried to teach kings how to rule in Deuteronomy 17:14–20, even though some did not listen. So, God set the example for us to pick up and become life-long learners in our ministries. Yes, you are equipped. Draw upon what you know and start there. Remember, education did not stop when you finished high school or college. It is continuous. Use your talents and gifts to prosper and build up your livelihood too. God did not provide these to us to horde. He gave them to us to share.

Media is wonderful when used correctly. This form of communication is by far the most innovative. Exploring media is one of the best things you can do for your ministry to reach multitudes. Your knowledge along with media will draw many because you have so much life to breathe into those who are hurting, or need an extra boost. Your creations will be worth sharing, and great for financial growth. I hope you will look at utilizing podcasts, audios, and videos with a new energy. If you look carefully, you can do these things with little, or no money. While searching, you may discover hidden talents you didn't know you had.

Part of you may be thrilled and frightened at the same time. Don't worry. It is just you, your computer, and God. You can mess up, sound silly, and scream, and no one listening but you and God. The point is you can learn to overcome fears and apprehensions about the unknown.

I join you and others in working for the best "boss" in the world. Ministry is what we do. It is exciting to know that our ministries are wide open reaching out to others. The great educator passes down his outline for ministry in 2 Corinthians 5:11–21. After reading these remarkable verses, your mission should be clearer. I learned we must carry on the tradition that Paul and others set for us by utilizing our intelligence and passion to live for Christ and to reach the lost.

I look forward to reaching the summit of the mountain of education and media with you as you discover your immeasurable God-given talent and intense enthusiasm to embrace your next assignment. You, your life, and your ministry will spring and bloom to life.

Mastering the Mountain
- Use "wordly" wisdom to expand your impact on others.
- God intends for us to use our knowledge for purpose and increase.
- Education, media and ministry are powerful when woven together.

MINISTRY BEYOND THE FOUR WALLS

Ashlei N. Evans

This chapter focuses on conquering the cultural mountain of education. The reader will gain wisdom and insight as it pertains to overcoming the trials and tribulations of education. Readers will be guided through the process of recognizing the influence of the mountain, adjusting their perspective, and understanding their life is a ministry.

ABOUT THIS AUTHOR

Ashlei N. Evans

Ashlei N. Evans is a Houston native, born and reared in Texas. She is an educator within the public school system and founder of The Ash Exchange, an organization geared towards embracing the brokenhearted, educating the lost, and empowering the hopeless. She graduated recently with her Doctorate in Literacy in which she raised awareness of biblical literacy through her dissertation. She hopes to expand The Ash Exchange to improve education both in America and Africa.

Even in Ashlei's leisure time of enjoying her dog, music, writing, and Nollywood (Nigerian movies), her heart remains steadfast in the desire to educate and enrich others.

Connect with this author and speaker for your next event:
Website: *www.TheAshExchange.com*
Facebook: *www.Facebook.com/DrAshleiNEvans*
Email: *AshleiNEvans@gmail.com*

More from Ashlei N. Evans
> *Biblical Literacy in a Secular World: Secondary Students' Perceptions of the Influence of Biblical Practices on Academic Achievement*

Available Services
> Inspirational and motivational speaking (e.g., faith-based, leadership, identity, spiritual gifts)
> Life coaching, mentoring, and educational consulting

MINISTRY BEYOND THE FOUR WALLS

Ashlei N. Evans

"You are the light of the world. A city that is set on a hill cannot be hidden. Nor do they light a lamp and put it under a basket, but on a lampstand, and it gives light to all *who are* in the house. Let your light so shine before men, that they may see your good works and glorify your Father in heaven."
—Matthew 5:14–16 NKJV

According to the late Nelson Mandela, "Education is the most powerful weapon which you can use to change the world." Obviously, his statement is true as educational wars have been fought for many years with our schools being the battle grounds. The purpose of education has been altered and much of its focus has gotten lost in politics, money, and standardized tests. As an educator, it is disheartening to see what education has become, but as a believer in Christ I know that even in the midst of darkness God has chosen me to be a light. We all are called to one of the seven cultural mountains, but in order for us to be effective and master these mountains, we must recognize the influence of the mountain, adjust our perspective, and understand that our life is ministry.

Education as a Mountain

Hosea 4:6 states, "My people are destroyed for lack of knowledge." I agree considering that one is not able to do better if they don't know what to do. With this unspoken truth, it becomes evident that education plays a significant role in the progression of society and personal development. Even Jesus understood the importance of education being that He is the ultimate teacher. The Bible is filled with teachings and instruction that Christ deemed necessary for our journey through life.

I recently completed my dissertation focusing on Biblical literacy and secondary students' perception on how it impacts their academic achievement. While gathering research on Biblical literacy I found that the foundation of many educational practices were rooted in religion. There were many cultural systems established based upon the Bible, as well as development in literacy and character skills. Speaking with older individuals, prayer used to be in schools, but eventually prayer was removed. Upon prayer being removed from schools, our education systems began to slowly collapse. Soon a lack of integrity seeped into the forefront and the system that once developed individuals began to tear them down. With the gradual decline in the success of education, more and more students consider it to be irrelevant. Sadly, many individuals don't see the correlation between education and the role it plays in their life.

Perspective is Everything

My brethren, count it all joy when you fall into various trials, knowing that the testing of your faith produces patience. But let patience have its perfect work, that you may be perfect and complete, lacking nothing (James 1:2–4 NKJV). God calls us to the very area that challenges yet liberates us the most. Often, and strategically, we are placed in areas where we are fought the most and in my case it is education. Academically, God graced me to always perform well, but there were many external factors that tried to drive me off course.

Financial burdens, loss of loved ones, and constant struggles to progress almost led me to leave education. During my first and second years of teaching, I was ready to quit. The long hours, the lack of structure, and the disrespect of adults and children, all contributed to me almost walking away from the very area God needed me to be. During this time, I gained a true understanding of the "fight or flight" concept. Initially, I was ready for flight, but God took me through a season of revelation where he showed me that I was to fight.

In 2012, I accepted a position at a school within a large district. I began in August and by October, I was the seventh teacher to resign. I questioned whether I made a mistake becoming a teacher. On my last day, I received a call back from another district to be a reading interventionist and that is when I was reminded that God needed me in education. I stayed in that position for a whole year with a 75% pay cut and an afterschool tutoring job to help cover expenses. I could not take on another full-time teaching job because the district I resigned from had a reputation of sanctioning teaching certificates. During that year, God showed me what was meant in James 1:2–4. I learned that my challenges within education were not to harm me, but to develop a level of patience within me that I would need while trying to conquer this mountain.

Your Life is a Ministry

The longer I'm in education the more God shows me what He is doing and what he desires to do in and through me. I've been privileged to work in affluent and urban schools only to find out that each has its own set of problems. In both environments, I found myself being a light to children and adults. The oppression of those the enemy used to attack me did not go away, but God always protected me and allowed me to reflect his love through my speech and actions. Eventually, I realized that my position in education was far more than just a way to pay bills.

My whole life had become a testament of God's grace, mercy, and love which paved the way for my life to be ministry. God is so strategic that he begins preparing us for our cultural mountain even in the earliest stages of our life. I think back to how teachers would often choose me to help students who struggled in their classes. As a student, I attended multiple schools of different ethnic and socioeconomic backgrounds. God has favored and accelerated me in the field of education by allowing me to attain my bachelors, masters, and now my doctoral degree in education by the age of 30. God even blessed me with the opportunity to develop teachers and even in that position, He still gives me the chance to speak life into students, teachers, administrators, and other district representatives. The journey has not been easy, but seeing the shift that's manifesting in education is all that matters.

Closing

A principal once told me that I would never succeed in public education because it was a "political beast." Honestly, she was partially right ... it is a political beast, but God knew what would happen and He has strategically positioned people in different areas of education to make a change. There are some things that God will highlight for us to cover in prayer and wait for Him to move, but then there are other areas where God wants to use us to bring about change. The tests and trials do not end, but remember our task is to reflect Christ and be the light of the world. Romans 12:9--21 shows us what being a true Christian looks like, but verse 12 specifically shows us how to persevere and continue to climb the mountain in spite of all the things that try to stop our progress. So, challenge yourself to always be "rejoicing in hope, patient in tribulation, continuing steadfastly in prayer" because God has equipped and empowered you to be a change agent of this world and transform culture.

Mastering the Mountain
- Recognize the influence of the mountain.
- Adjust your perspective.
- Understand your life is a ministry.

QUALIFIED FOR THE PURPOSE

Laneice McGee

The Lord had you in mind before the very foundation of the world, and with that, he has placed inside of you - a purpose, a reason, and a call. It's not forced upon you, but eagerly waiting to be fulfilled. The fact remains the same if God called you; he qualified you—not based on your perception of yourself, but based on his perception of you. In order to live the life he dreamed of when he created you, you must first accept the fact that he will use whom he pleases to complete his will. He does not have limits; and if he said it, he will supply your needs to sustain it.

ABOUT THIS AUTHOR

Laneice McGee

Armed with a Bachelor of Arts in Sociology and a Master of Science in Human Services, combined with extensive work experience, Laneice McGee is well qualified in her current role as the District Director for the Department of Workforce Development at the Waukesha, Ozaukee, and Washington County District (W.O.W.).

Laneice lets her motivating fun side shine through as she mentors youth who desire to start and manage their own business. Her inspiration doesn't stop there, she is also devoted to cultivating a positive self and body image in women through Big, Beautiful, and Blessed. In all of this, Laneice remains an active member of her community and church.

Connect with this author and speaker for your next event:
Website: *www.LaneiceMcGee.com*
Facebook: *www.Facebook.com/LaneiceM*
Email: *Info@LaneiceMcGee.com*

More from Laneice McGee
   Speak Your Peace (Anthology) Compiler: Jodine Basterash
   My Business, His Way (Forthcoming)

Available Services
   Inspirational / Motivational Speaking
   You are an Entrepreneur (Workshop on Getting Started)
   F.E.M.A. (Future Entrepreneurs Moving Ahead) founder
   Big, Beautiful & Blessed (co-founder)

QUALIFIED FOR THE PURPOSE

Laneice McGee

And do not be conformed to this world, but be transformed by the renewing of your mind, that you may prove what is that good and acceptable and perfect will of God.

—Romans 12:2 NKJV

As a man thinketh, so is he. What are your thoughts? How do you see yourself? Dig deep, ask these questions, and answer them truthfully. Do you see yourself in perfect peace? Do you see yourself as the head and not the tail? Do you see yourself as the lender and not the borrower? Do you see yourself as fruitful, with an abundant life? The issue is not *what* you see; it is *how* you see it. Your mind must be transformed to see yourself and your circumstances the way God sees them. He is not concerned about the *why* and the *how*; He is concerned about the posture of your heart and your level of faith in Him.

If we cannot honestly say that our mind has been transformed, it's time we take a step back and start to be intentional about our thoughts. If we want to know the will of God for our life, we need to start thinking like him; we need to start walking it out in faith; we need to know his voice so we can confirm his will. It is a process. It takes discipline. We have to stop in order to go.

I had been so busy in my life working, running a business, family, friends, and other responsibilities, that I had not really taken a moment of solitude and rest in God. Although

I did the lip service of repentance and my heart was sincere, I had not allowed my mind to be renewed or transformed. I went to church I heard the Word, I shouted and praised the Lord but left and went right back to my busy and unfruitful life. You see, if I really took time to stop the constant, futile activities, I would have to deal with my divorce; I would have to deal with my hurts, I would have to deal with my disappointments. What if I did not hear God's voice but only the echoes of my regrets? I wanted the fruit of the land, but I did not want the digging and toiling that goes before the fruit is produced. No matter how busy I appeared, deep down in my heart I knew God had more. I recognized that God had a divine purpose for my life and in order to receive it, I had to have the courage to face, deal, and release that which I thought I had control of, but never really did. So, if you are reading this and you struggle to know what the purpose of God is in your life, I am suggesting that you need to get quiet so you can hear. You need to release your will so you can submit to his.

Steps to Transform Your Mind to Hear the Will of God
1. Get quiet, make time everyday to pray and listen to the voice of God.
2. Study the Word so that your thoughts will line up to the Word of God.
3. Surround yourself with others that you know and they proclaim they are living God's will for their life. Glean from them.

Make it a habit to check your thoughts daily. When you change your thoughts, you can change your life. Just like you decide what you are going to eat, where you are going to go, and what you are wearing for the day, decide what you are going to think. That is how much control we need to have over our thoughts. We must immediately reject any unhealthy thought, and replace it with a promise of God. Whatever is nurtured will grow, so don't dwell on that which is unhealthy. Furthermore, that which you plant you will reap. So I ask you, what has been growing in the garden of your heart? I challenge you in the area of shaping your thoughts. Start writing down how you see yourself and your circumstance and then write down what God says about those things. Every time one of those thoughts come up, you are prepared to attack it with the truth of the Word of God. In order to walk in what God has qualified you for, you must first see and think according to whose you are. Who do you belong to? Are you acting like it in your thoughts and actions? Remind yourself that the one who resides in you is greater than the one that is in the world.

Once you have mastered managing your thoughts, you need to understand that if God called you, he will qualify you. Stop questioning if you have been called. Stop questioning why you have been called. First of all, embrace the knowledge that you have been designed with a purpose in mind. God did not create anyone for no reason at all. Secondly, leave the reason (the "why me") up to God. Don't waste those precious brain cells on telling God what you can't do and providing him suggestions of who could do it. Lastly, God did not ask you, nor will he allow your faithlessness to intrude on his greatness. If God called you, then he is responsible to provide. Be like David in the Scriptures who cried out to God that he (God) would fulfill his purpose in David (Psalm 57:2).

We must be confident in understanding that nothing and no one can stand in the way of God's purpose over our lives.

Weapons may form, but they will not prosper (Isaiah 54:17). Hence, knowing this, we can stop focusing on the reason why God called us; he has taken care of that. Therefore, we must be diligent in preparing. He has called you, now work it. Yes, you have natural talents, but perfect that which you have been entrusted with. If you have a child, you don't want to send them to just any daycare or school. It's great that the teacher has a natural gift to work with children, but you want the best for yours, so you want that teacher to be certified, and who has probably taken CPR classes, and so on. You want them to have honed their skills. We should be doing the same thing as entrepreneurs. Stay hungry to grow, don't surrender to what is comfortable, when you were created to achieve the better. Why settle for good when we know from the Word of God that great is an option. Always be prepared for the next opportunity God will bring your way. The Bible states that without faith works is dead (James 2:17). So once we give up debating the why and even surrender the how, then we can operate in faith being confident because we are not only gifted, but we are competent, diligent, and effective.

In closing, I want to encourage you to release those thoughts which no longer serve your future. God's will for your life can be revealed, but you must first be silent and still to hear. He will not force you to receive but will honor a willing heart. It may take time, but be consistent, knowing that God will take care of you, and no good thing will he withhold. So, don't allow your short-term desires to rob you of your long-term dreams. God has already qualified you for the purpose. He will fulfill that which he has promised. The favor of God rests upon your life, get prepared to walk through that door—be it through schooling, training, seminars, mastermind groups or wherever the Lord leads.

The mountain of education is a gift; it creates a platform to sharpen your skills and abilities and share that which you were given with others. In this classroom, the head master has already qualified you.

Mastering the Mountain
- It's not your responsibility to worry about why God called you; it's your responsibility to trust the process.
- Those whom God calls, he qualifies.
- Don't just wait for the favor, be prepared for it.

FROM EDUCATOR TO ENTREPRENEUR

Beverly Walthour

Education is one thing that can never be taken away from you. With it, you can change the world. Because of this, it's imperative that we have educators who are passionate about education and have the resources needed to be effective and impact the next generation!

ABOUT THIS AUTHOR

Beverly Walthour

Strategist, trainer, author, business owner, educator: Beverly Walthour. Beverly has created a successful program to teach business strategies to women coaches and consultants on how to create consistent clients and income within 12 weeks. This former middle school math teacher has successfully started four businesses of her own. Beverly is truly a spiritually-minded, generous, and fun-loving entrepreneur who cares enough for others to share her wisdom and experience through a variety of podcast interviews, online television, radio, and magazines.

Connect with this author and speaker for your next event:
Website: *www.BeverlyWalthour.com/*
Facebook: *www.Facebook.com/CoachBeverlyWalthour*
Email: *Beverly@BeverlyWalthour.com*

More from Beverly Walthour
12 Places to Find Your Next High-paying Clients in Your Coaching or Consulting Business

Available Services
Consulting
Inspirational / motivational "How-to" Speaker Topics
for Coaches and Consultants:
Starting Your Own Business; Eliminating Fear; and
Using Social Media to Grow Your Business

FROM EDUCATOR TO ENTREPRENEUR

Beverly Walthour

Train up a child in the way he should go, And when he is old he will not depart from it.

—Proverbs 22:6 NKJV

As educators, we are entrusted with God's most precious creations—children. In addition to parents, educators help lay the foundation that students use later in life. Although many of us see Proverbs 22:6 as a scripture for parents, as an educator, I took it to heart.

As a former middle school educator of 14 years, I was blessed to have touched the lives of thousands of students. Getting a good education was always important to me, because I knew it would be my ticket to anything I wanted to do. It would allow me to get out of the small town I grew up in, and to see the world. My journey as an educator started when I was a young girl. I always knew I would be a teacher. When I was in elementary school, I would come home from school and teach my baby sister everything I learned that day. As I got older, I never shook that feeling to teach, however, I also started thinking about learning about business.

As a high school senior, I applied for two scholarships. One was for business and one was for education. I won the education one and it sealed the deal for me. I chose to attend the University of Georgia because it had one of the best schools of education. I was fortunate to have had some of the best professors and be surrounded by other students who were on fire for education as well. I remember one of my professors telling us we should have a goal of becoming Teacher of the Year within five years of becoming a teacher. That challenge always stuck with me.

Upon graduation, I chose to work in a district comprised of mostly minority students. During my time there, I was fortunate enough to have others see leadership in me when I did not see it in myself. Due to this, I held a number of leadership roles which enabled me to impact the lives of even more students. Six years into teaching, I achieved the challenge my professor had given us. I was named Teacher of the Year!

However, around this time, I was starting to become disillusioned with the field of education. Laws were being passed by people who've never set foot inside a classroom, the flexibility in how content was being taught was being taken away from teachers, parents and teachers weren't feeling supported, and students were being affected by the changes. I no longer felt I was being effective. One year after being named, Teacher of the Year, I left the classroom to pursue entrepreneurship. However, I knew that I was not leaving education behind. There was too much that needed to be done. I just had to figure out how to do it in a way that would bring about the most effective change.

It used to be that after high school you either went to college, work, or the military. Now, one more option is available to students right after high school and that is being an entrepreneur. With this new option, it is imperative that we teach students about entrepreneurship. This is something that can start in early elementary school in which we teach students how to identify areas of strengths for them and how they can leverage it to create a business of their own. This is usually something done in households in which a parent or relative is also an entrepreneur. However, for those students who do not have this in their home environment, often, they don't learn about these things until much later in life (if they learn about it at all).

It is important to offer these sorts of programs in all schools so that students are exposed to this early on. This can be in the form of actual curriculum that is taught during the school day and/or before or after school programs. As educators, God puts his most precious creations in our hands. We must ensure we are providing them with every opportunity to be successful. It is important that when they graduate from high school or college, that we have prepared them as much as we possibly can to be global thinkers and leaders.

As an educator, having a background in entrepreneurship is a great way to enhance this experience for our students. Unless you have been an entrepreneur, it is unlikely you will ever understand that experience. Not only would being an entrepreneur help them with their students, but it is also a great way to generate multiple streams of revenue. In this day and age, it has become critical to have more than one source of income so you can still manage if a source is eliminated.

I think one of the best things that enriched me as an educator is when I decided to become an entrepreneur. Having that experience enabled me to share experiences and ideas with students which I could not do before. For instance, I had a student who struggled academically in many of his classes except mine. One day we were talking, and I asked him what he wanted to do after high school. He said all he was interested in was skateboarding. I asked him had he ever thought about opening his own business based on his passion for skateboarding. This immediately caught his interest. He was doubtful at first, but after reminding him about a popular music artist who has products for those who skateboard, he was convinced he could do it too. We actually brainstormed a few ideas that he could start working on as a middle school student. I would not have felt confident in having that conversation with him without my own entrepreneurial background.

One of my goals as an entrepreneur is to start a non-profit that will put entrepreneurial programs and courses in our K-12 schools. As a former classroom teacher, I understand how the system works and how important it is for teachers to be a part of this process. Not only will these show our students how to develop an entrepreneurial mindset, but also our educators.

There are many educators who desire to start their own businesses, but do not know how. They have so many skills that will serve them well as entrepreneurs. With the boom in online businesses, the possibilities are endless. Online opportunities provide educators with the chance to bring additional income into their homes and for those who want to move beyond the classroom, this can enable them to do so. Gone are the days where people spend 30-40 years on a job and their only option is to retire. For those of you who are in your season as an educator, you are responsible for providing the best possible education for these students God has entrusted in your care.

In the meantime, also use that time to explore entrepreneurial opportunities. Know that God has you in the field of education for a reason. If pursuing entrepreneurship is something you want to do as an educator, below are a few tips to help you get started so you can make a powerful impact:

- Ensure that you pray over yourself and your students each day and ask God to keep you open for opportunities to grow as an educator and an entrepreneur.

- Research various online businesses you can start based on things you are passionate about (both inside and outside the classroom). There are countless opportunities online for you to teach people courses and programs in your areas of interest.
- Reach out to others you know who have started businesses. As a business strategist for female coaches and consultants, I help women in this area all the time.
- It is very feasible to continue working as an educator as you grow your business (especially if it is online). If you decide to remain in education, you can use your business as additional income. If you decide to pursue entrepreneurship full-time, you can build a nice financial cushion before transitioning.

As I reflect over the past 10 years I've spent as both a successful educator and entrepreneur, I've learned many things. I will close with the three key things in the *Mastering the Mountain* section.

Mastering the Mountain

- Prayer is so important to your success. If God has placed something in your heart, he will bring it to pass. You just have to remain faithful and take action.
- It is imperative to have multiple streams of revenue coming into your household. Some of the best ways to do this is to have passive income (e.g., selling digital products, investing)
- Being an educator is one of the most rewarding careers you can ever have. You have the opportunity to leave a life-long positive and impactful impression on a child.

Media

There is so much chatter these days about things that don't matter at all or things that only carry temporary worth. Media covers all kinds of mass communication regardless of whether it is pubic speaking, written materials such as books and magazines, or digital communications, e.g., eBooks. As believers, we should dominate this mountain. We are the ones with the best message everyone *needs* to hear.

Gain insight from the following authors:

Onika Shirley 113

Leslie M. Dillard 121

THE POWER OF MEDIA WILL LET YOUR LIGHT SHINE

Onika Shirley

Your sphere of influence can be expanded beyond your imagination if you stand firm on your media mountain and take hold of the platforms that are now available unto you. Speak up and speak loud because 'Action Speaks Volume.'

ABOUT THIS AUTHOR

Onika Shirley

Onika Shirley is a sponge for soaking up new information and experiences. She is the founder and CEO of Action Speaks Volume, Inc., she operates Action Speaks Volume Orphanage Home and Foundation in India, and recently started writing her own column in *Ordinary People* magazine. Onika holds a bachelor's in business accounting and master's in business administration. She is currently working on her doctorate in Christian Counseling.

Onika's faith in God has given her an unstoppable mindset. "You can do whatever it is you want to do despite the odds against you."

Connect with this author and speaker for your next event:
Website: *http://ActionSpeaksVolum.com/*
Facebook: *http://Facebook.com/ActionSpeaksVolume/*
Email: *ActionSpeaksVolume@gmail.com*

More from Onika Shirley
  Women We Must Stand Strong
  Her Prayers "Prayers for the Deeply Wounded"
  Purpose Shakers: Women Who Rise to the Call of Purpose
    "Purpose Driven, No Matter What!"

Available Services
  Action Takers Mentoring Program (and coaching)
  Financial Fitness Consulting
  Inspirational/Motivational Speaking
    Topics: procrastination and life skills

THE POWER OF MEDIA WILL LET YOUR LIGHT SHINE

Onika Shirley

And the Lord said, Behold, the people is one, and they have all one language; and this they begin to do: and now nothing will be restrained from them, which they have imagined to do.

—Genesis 11:6 KJV

The moment I realized how powerful media could be, I changed my perspective about social media and other media platforms. There was the power of media communication right from the very beginning of time. Genesis 11:6 (KJV) tells us, "And the Lord said, Behold, the people is one, and they have all one language; and this they begin to do: and now nothing will be restrained from them, which they have imagined to do." The media mountain in the Bible resembles a similar model today through the power of the World Wide Web, social media, and satellite communication. Information and messages which used to take hours and sometimes days can now be communicated across the world in a matter of seconds. I have come to realize that without the media mountain, arts and entertainment, business, education, family, government, and the religion mountain would be "scattered." Think about how limited we would be in our communication today without media platforms. As entrepreneurs and business partners, we use the media to communicate internally and externally. We also use the media to market and advertise our products and services. As individuals, social media, podcast, blogs, radio broadcasts, and websites are used for entertainment and to disseminate messages to sustain relevancy and to create a well-known brand.

Social media and other media platforms are everywhere so you can take the world along with you wherever you go. As a business owner, I discovered that media could be used to my advantage. Individuals and businesses have seen the benefits of the media and decided to take action. The media mountain for me personally—the business of Action Speaks Volume, initially started as a simple means of staying in the know, in addition to social networking, and relationship building. Today, it has evolved into a creative and innovative digital marketing strategy for the business. We must move with the times or drown in the deep waves of competition and isolation. I took advantage of media as it pertains to many parts of my business in order to start engaging my audience and to give them what they wanted in a timely fashion. Media has allowed me to go to places I've never been to reach people I've never seen. I speak to you today from personal experience. I host a live weekly radio broadcast heard in almost 160 countries, operate Action Speak Volume Foundation, and an Orphanage Home in India via social media. I produce blogs for The Huffington Post, Action Speaks Volume, Inc., and Woman Boss Magazine. These life experiences qualify me to discuss this mountain even though just a while back, I had no idea how to reach my target market. Media is the era of this time and this particular mountain matters. The media mountain matters to individuals and businesses because it grants us access to another level of exposure. It grants us access to people, places, and things we never would've imagined. We have newspapers, televisions, radios, and the internet. Can you imagine going back to not having the access that you now have today? Media has opened my eyes and my reach.

Now, pay close attention to the many different forms of media and try to understand how powerful and significant media are in our time and to the competitiveness of businesses. I find it really hard to think about operating a business today without the internet. I think it will be hard to remain competitive. Consumers are all about pointing and clicking. My associates and people in my circle love the convenience of the internet. Businesses have seen such great benefits of doing things online versus having to do everything up close and eye-to-eye personal. Consumers and clients purchase travel, make restaurant reservations, and electronically negotiate and sign sales contracts all online. Can you now see how media has had an impact on business? Business online has been the driving force for other businesses having to close their doors and stores of brick and mortar having become obsolete. Social media alone has changed how businesses search, reach, interact with customers, intrigue curiosity, and offer products and services. Businesses today also use media to communicate with internal employees and for the purposes of high value marketing. I am talking about some of the most popular platforms of social media today like Facebook, Twitter, Instagram, and LinkedIn. Media drives business and the best way for businesses to get competitive and remain competitive is to fully embrace the Media Mountain of social media. If a business decides not to incorporate social media channels and others media platforms into their business they are not leveraging their potential earnings and they are limiting their reach and sphere of potential influence. I think not using media, over time, can have a negative impact on the influence of a business and it will leave one, regrettably, far behind.

Businesses see the challenges and opportunities of this facet of media due to business transparency and engagement. Between press releases and the internet, privacy now only lives in days gone by. We are also well past the fresh-off-the-press campaigns to communicate with customers and clients from behind the scene. People want to know the owners and desire to have a relationship with the businesses with whom they are doing business. Media tends to force relationships with customers and requires more answers to open-ended questions and concerns. Transparency is real and media is changing the way we do business.

Opportunities
- Businesses can now make connections on social media without spending a lot of money and make connections a lot quicker.
- Businesses can convert from "large campaigns" and spending millions of dollars on traditional material to small acts like following and hitting likes.
- Businesses can show their personal professional side to consumers and clients versus controlling their non-humorous images.

Challenges
- Consumers will build relationships with competition simply because they now have access.
- Businesses can become a target to predators and scammers.
- Businesses need to know where their customers are. Sometimes, this can be a challenge.

As a business owner, I can most certainly see how media has influenced my own life. Media influence is not by accident, it is intentional. I have found from personal experience that media changes our mindsets and it has an influence on our thinking. When advertising, it is deliberate, targeted and it's powerful. This is good news because media can be very positive and the vehicle one will need to move to the next level. As I started to use the media more, my following increased substantially and sometimes my own thoughts were influenced by the media. I found it very easy to meet people all over the world simply by being present and consistent. Social media allowed me to expand my business globally by being open, while also gaining additional exposure. I remember being a part of a group on Facebook and it led to a connection with a woman in Jamaica. Over the period of a few months, we communicated, shared ideas, and business strategies which eventually led into me attending a global mastermind which she was hosting. My attendance opened the door for future opportunities and connections with so many other people and businesses.

I am using media as a positive influence in people lives here in the midst of a negative world while spreading the goodness of my Lord and Savior Jesus Christ. I show up consistently in a positive manner to inspire, motivate, and empower people all over the world. I have also helped many to come to know Christ and accept him as their Lord and Savior. The media mountain can be powerful and positive and if used appropriately, people can reach individuals all over the world—lives can be changed and businesses can explode. I am conveying messages and spreading a word daily via Facebook live, a weekly radio broadcast, and magazine features. It is so important to have a vehicle to drive your messages, products, and services to the next destination. Once you get there you can show others just exactly how it is done. I show up in the marketplace by living the life I coach and talk about.

The things you are afraid of doing—God has a hedge of protection around you. The people you are afraid to address—God knows the approach you need to take to be effective. The audience you are unsure of—God has (and is) the answer. The rejection you intensely fear—God loves you so much and he promises to never leave you alone. Have faith in God and know that he is working on your behalf.

Stand firm on your mountain, be open and honest with God. Stand firm on your mountain, and allow Him to use your voice. Be full of wisdom downloaded from Him. Take a firm stand on your belief about the media, meditate on truth, be humble, and remain open to God's counsel.

Mastering the Mountain
- Media can be used to market and advertise our products and services.
- Media can go in places and reach people we may never see face to face.
- Media can be used as a positive influence in the lives of people in the midst of a negative world.

Don't Bring Me No Bad News

Leslie M. Dillard

Bad news, we come to expect it. Just like sex, it sells. Disasters, military interventions all sold to the public through effective media marketing; molding and shaping our thoughts until we don't know what to think anymore or in some cases how to think. I'm in control, or am I?

About this Author

Leslie M. Dillard

Born in Taiwan to military parents, Leslie has been writing poetry for years. Serving in her 35th year in the Army, retirement is on her mind. She is an avid golfer and has been involved in youth ministry for 20 + years and is considered the biggest kid in the church. Fun-loving as she may be, her love for her Savior drove her back to school to pursue a doctorate program in strategic leadership (Ecclesial) in the spring of 2018.

Connect with this author and speaker for your next event:
Website: *www.GodFirstProductionsLLC.com*
Facebook: *God First Productions*
Email: *GodFirstProdLLC@gmail.com*

More from Leslie M. Dillard
   From the Situation to the Destination: Poems and Meditations to Provide Encouragement for Life's Tough Times

Available Services
   Motivational Speaker Topics:
      Mentorship, Leadership, Self Esteem,
   Spoken Word Artist and Playwright:
      Personalized Poetry Creationist
   Workshop:
      Developing Spoken Word for Praise and Worship

Don't Bring Me No Bad News

Leslie M. Dillard

How beautiful upon the mountains are the feet of him who brings good news, who proclaims peace, who brings glad tidings of good things, who proclaims salvation, who says to Zion, "Your God reigns!"

—Isaiah 52:7 NKJV

The media mountain is the trumpet for all other mountains of influence. Our perceptions are shaped by what we see and hear. Influencing positive change in today's culture must be done through the efficient and effective use of media and shaping its sometimes contentious relationship with the public.

In August 2005, Katrina, a category 5 hurricane, devastated the Louisiana coast. As I sat glued to my TV watching with the rest of the world, and as the levee system failed and Lake Pontchartrain overtook the city of New Orleans, I knew it would be only a matter of time before the Department of Defense would be called to support. Those around me, frustrated and angry, began to ask how the Federal Government could let this happen. Why had we let one of the nation's most iconic cities drown? The news reporting perpetuated these questions, and more. Not once did any news anchor describe the process of receiving federal support. If they had, many would not have been so critical of FEMA (Federal Emergency Management Agency) and other federal agencies that eventually were requested to support and respond to such a tragic disaster. What many didn't understand was that the Federal Government must be invited, requested by the governor. All disasters are local. According to the U.S. Constitution, neither FEMA nor the Federal Government have the authority to order evacuations unless the President invokes the insurrection act and waives posse comitatus,[1] a fact not discussed in any news reporting of Katrina.

As a 35-year member of the armed forces and subject matter expert in defense support to civil authorities, I have participated in a number of disaster responses which uniquely qualifies me to share how the media impacts public perception on disaster response and military operations. Gone are the days when a journalist would take hours or even days to develop a story, check facts, and report. With today's technology and access, everyone with a camera phone is a reporter and it only takes seconds to become part of a news cycle. When conducting military operations, leadership is keenly aware of what we call the CNN effect, which is defined as the influence news media has on politics and political decisions. With respect to natural disasters, it is the effect broadcast images have on the public psyche and how quickly and completely the government does or does not respond. During Katrina, it was very rare that we heard how well FEMA or DoD (Department of Defense) was doing in response to the disaster declaration. The pictures of overcrowded conditions at the stadium, looting and slow response to issues in low income and minority communities like the 9th Ward perpetuated the perception that the government had abandoned the citizens of New Orleans.

---

[1] Posse comitatus: a type of common law in which authorized law officers, e.g., county sheriff has the legal authority to recruit suitable persons to assist in enforcing the law and order in a given area.

So what do you say? Why do I care what the media reports and whether it's rooted in truth or not? Because the mountain of media is the conduit for all other mountains to connect with the public, it behooves us as Christians to get a grip on this mountain! Today's insatiable thirst for expedient information can only be quenched through effective use of the media. Matthew 28:19 tells us to go and teach all nations and baptize them in the name of the Father, the Son and the Holy Ghost. To follow through on this command we must utilize all forms of media from social platforms such as Twitter and Facebook to the "old school" newspaper and magazine. We have work to do for the kingdom and we cannot be effective if we don't utilize all the tools available to us. When used effectively and truthfully, media itself can be a powerful ally in reclaiming the media mountain.

The BP oil spill was an example of how very public disagreements can impact a response. When political and business agendas are played out in the media, justice can be delayed for those affected by the disaster. BP continued to run commercials detailing their commitment to ensuring the Gulf was restored, a positive spin but the back-story of very public law suits and hundreds of families losing generational businesses was not so positive. Egos and financial bottom lines became the priority as those responsible for the spill pointed fingers at each other, not wanting to accept responsibility for the massive cleanup or the bill associated with it. The economic loss as a result of the oil spill was devastating, but coverage of the Obama's administration taking a plunge to demonstrate that the gulf was safe and open for business, sent a positive message to the nation. This very public display by the leader of the free world helped shape a positive perception and provided a much-needed moral boost for the region.

The most recent barrage of natural disasters saw positive reporting in comparison to Katrina. On the heels of racial tension in Charlottesville, a very different picture emerged from Houston as the city pulled together in the wake of Hurricane Harvey. Information was distributed in a timely manner, citizens heeded the warnings, and neighbors helped each other to recover. Even when the media falsely reported that Joel Osteen didn't open the doors of the church, that false report quickly died when he addressed the concern on national TV. When there are misunderstandings about processes and how operations work during a disaster, it can lead to negative and erroneous information being posted and reported. The enemy loves confusion—God is not the author of confusion. If you become a victim of misinformation, "nip it in the bud" right then. Confront, correct, and move on.

The media today thrives and survives on bad news and sensationalism to ensure viewers are tuned in. There is such a steady stream of bad news these days that many stop watching the news to avoid depression! What kind of legacy are we leaving for our children, with respect to public and media relations? How can we take the mountain of media and secure it for the Kingdom of God?

First, we must recognize that our media today does not always concern itself with truth. This is a competitive arena and issuing a retraction is part of the business, just get the story out. I believe, if you don't stand for the truth then you're standing for a lie. Are you a defender of truth?

Secondly, we must be courageous and hold those reporting falsehoods accountable. If we don't challenge it, they won't change it. Will you correct the wrong or let it pass?

Thirdly, Public Relations 101—ensure your message is received as intended. Often the media gets the message wrong because we haven't conveyed it correctly. The current fight over kneeling during the National Anthem is not about the flag or military members—it's about bringing attention to the racial inequality in the nation. So how did we get to this point? The initial messaging was not clear and when it was portrayed incorrectly, the "movement" didn't immediately clear the air. There is no getting the genie back in the bottle once it's out.

Today's headlines are full of bad news and misinformation. It is rare that we hear those heartwarming, feel-good stories we heard in the past. Media has the ability to change our perception and therefore over time, evil has become good, the truth has become a twisted collage of facts, opinion and misinformation. The continual bombardment of negative media and misrepresentation feed the public's insatiable appetite for stories that shock and tear down versus inform and build up. Spin and fake news have become the operative words on the mountain of media and if we as Christians are to take this mountain, we must take responsibility for correcting what is wrong and holding those reporting the news and distribution outlets accountable when they get it wrong.

Public, media relations, by its very definition, implies there is a relationship between the public and the media. We can change the narrative and shape this relationship as we move forward to conquer this mountain. It won't be easy but it can and must be done in order for us to control the other mountains of influence. We can use the very same tools the enemy uses to manipulate to educate and stimulate positive action in climbing the mountain of media. The enemy isn't just going to give us this mountain, we will have to take it by force. Are you the feet bringing good news? Are you the feet proclaiming peace? Are you the feet bringing good tidings?

Are you proclaiming salvation? Are you ready and willing to take the mountain of media? If so, don't bring me no bad news!

Mastering the Mountain

- In order to take the mountain of media and secure it for the kingdom of God we must recognize that our media today does not always concern itself with truth. This is a competitive arena and issuing a retraction is part of the business, just get the story out. If you don't stand for the truth then you're standing for a lie! Are you a defender of truth?
- We must be courageous and hold those reporting falsehoods accountable. If we don't challenge it, they won't change it. Will you correct the wrong or let it pass?
- Public Relations 101—ensure your message is received as intended. The media gets the message wrong because we haven't conveyed it correctly. Let's do our part to set the record straight.

Arts & Entertainment

For many of us, we love the arts and we love to be entertained with music, sports, you name it and we want more. For the most part, there's nothing wrong with that. However, God is calling us to something more meaningful than just being entertained. He's calling us to make a difference on this mountain. What can we do to influence this mountain? What can *you* do as a believer?

Gain insight from the following authors:

Wesliane Marie Kidd 131

Tanya E. Lawrence 137

HOW MANY WAYS CAN I GIVE PRAISE?

Wesliane Marie Kidd

It is a new day and we can praise God in just about any setting imaginable. Go to your quiet place, imagine a blank canvas. Put it on your easel, close your eyes and let the Holy Spirit guide you. By the end of this chapter, you will be surprised to see the beauty you have created.

ABOUT THIS AUTHOR

Wesliane Marie Kidd

Wesliane is what one might call both down-to-earth and multifaceted, rolled into one fun-loving bundle. A native of Louisiana, she has lived the past several years in Wisconsin and has had the opportunity to perform with the Ethiopian Theater in Louisiana.

While Wesliane considers herself a blessed, aspiring missionary, it is apparent that her love for people paints her as a true missionary. Part of Wesliane's ministry is revealed as she is licensed in both cosmetology and early childcare. She has also served on the board of directors in policy council for Head Start and served as a parent advocate for the Children Services Society and Lutheran Service. She delights in service to God through her work with the children's choir and youth activities.

Connect with this author and speaker for your next event:
Facebook: *Wesliane Kidd-Aguillard*
Email: *ILuvWes40@hotmail.com*

More from Wesliane Marie Kidd
　　English as a Second Language Instruction (Spanish)

Available Services
　　Teacher and Trainer:
　　　　The Art of Praise Dancing
　　　　How to Get Children and Youth Involved in Church
　　Wedding Planner
　　Travel Consultant and Owner: Simplywes Travel Agency

HOW MANY WAYS CAN I GIVE PRAISE?

Wesliane Marie Kidd

Thou art my God, and I will praise thee: thou art my God, I will exalt thee. O give thanks unto the Lord; for he is good: for his mercy endureth for ever.

—Psalms 118:28–29 KJV

Diagnosed with breast cancer at age 30 and again at 39 one may tend towards giving up. Why not? That was the beginning of a myriad of health problems I would endure for years, even till this day. Do you understand that pain when you have a small child to raise? None of us are promised tomorrow. Most of us think we don't know how to praise God if we are not a preacher, first lady, evangelist, or hold some other position we deem as an important role in the church. Well, you know the old saying, "Get in where you fit in"? I'm going to show you some places that you can fit in that are just as important as the others.

Pick Up Your Brush, the Canvas Awaits You

We may start at the bottom of this mountain but together we will reach the top. We will be strong and praise God because he is good. Have you sat in church and wanted to do more, but were too shy or thought that you were not good enough or didn't fit in? You are not the first and won't be the last. Not everyone praises in the same way, nor should they. I used to look at what I called "the prayer warriors" up front in church praying and I would say to myself, "Wow, I wish I could do that." That was not my calling. I love to sing, who said you have to sing in the choir to praise God through song? When you are in your home, car or anywhere you feel like singing a gospel song, know that you are giving God praise. Why do you think when you do that sometimes the Holy Spirit comes upon you and you may start to cry, shout, or just get excited? Because that is the way you might connect with God himself. God doesn't care if you are on key, off key, or no one can find your key. He only cares about your heart.

Let's Dance

Some of us like to dance. Praise dance is a form of art. Who better to dance for than God? The Holy Spirit is so powerful. You are never too old or too young to dance for God. That is one of the beautiful things about dance. Don't ever let anyone stop you from getting your praise dance on. That is something I enjoy doing and let me tell you it was about fifteen years between me and the next closest person to my age on the praise team. I was the oldest one out there. I am sure I was the only one aching after that but it was worth it to me. Praise dancing is also used a lot in the market place now. They are being done at conferences, weddings, parks or at any occasion that people want to be blessed with dance. It has become one of the fastest growing ministries in the church world.

With One or One Hundred One—Just Sing

Singing by one's self to God is good, but there is nothing wrong with singing with a group. The beauty of it is that you can sing with the church choir, quartet, solo, or start a group of your own. There is a strong market for all the above out here now. If you feel like you want to join any of these, do it. Don't let the naysayers hold you back. Remember that God has not given us a spirit of fear. If you are doing it because you feel like this will make your relationship with God better, then go for it. If you are shy and want to sing, join the choir.

Praise God Every Day

If you like to write poems, paint pictures, do some kind of sculpture, or even play an instrument those are all good too. In today's world, social media has taken over our lives and the lives of our children. We have to take back our lives and the lives of our children. One day at a time, one step at a time. Whatever type of music your children like, there is a Christ-centered version of it. If they like rap go out and buy some gospel rap. Now the best way to get them to listen to it is just put it on and learn the words to it. Don't let on that you got this for them. If you start singing it like you were singing a gangster rap song they might look at you like you're crazy at first but start enjoying it and before you know it they will be trying to out sing you. It just takes a little creativity on your part. We have to do things with our children and youth that they will enjoy to keep them interested. They too need to be equipped with all the tools so they will be able to praise God as the spirit leads them. No matter what you go through in life or when the adversities come, there is always a way you can give praise. It lies within you. Don't ever let anyone stop you from praising in your own way. God loves all of us the same. We are all his children.

I hope you can see the splendor and glory of your canvas. We are all beautiful and wonderfully made. Keep your canvas close and show it to the world. I hope you are able to help someone else paint their beautiful picture.

Mastering the Mountain

- Never be afraid to try something new. Praising God is not hard to do.
- When you realize that you have been praising him in some form or fashion, but no one ever pointed out to you that you were doing it already, take that leap of faith and expand on what you know now.
- Don't ever let anyone stop you from praising in your own way.

#SocialSuicide

Tanya E. Lawrence

We live in a day and age where our social skills are now being defined by a hashtag (#), tweet, instant message, emoji, or a few thumbs up or down. Social media has reached a pinnacle of success that affects every facet of our lives. Its boundaries are becoming limitless and have become the most prominent vehicle of how our society, family, and business, functions. No longer is social media just a vice to keep us entertained, but it has now become the driving force for all we do and think. Will we climb this mountain with ease or will it come with much hurt?

ABOUT THIS AUTHOR

Tanya E. Lawrence

Tanya Lawrence is truly a many-sided author, who is fun, educated, and spiritually grounded. Her fun side loves sweet tea, gummy bears, and traveling to exotic places. Having earned both a bachelor's and a master's degree in business management, plus a master's degree in management information systems, she now serves as an executive assistant for a large corporation.

Most importantly, Tanya has a passion for her Savior, Jesus Christ. She demonstrates this in her faithfulness to her church as she serves on the praise team and serves as the secretary/treasurer for her church's district. But nothing keeps her as grounded as when she's teaching the two to six-year-olds in Sunday school. Tanya's unique personality keeps her fan base ever growing.

Connect with this author and speaker for your next event:
　　Facebook:　*http://Facebook.com/TanyaLawrence/*
　　Email:　　 *cottonpatchpg@gmail.com*

More from Tanya E. Lawrence:
　　Priceless (a ministry in development devoted to helping others see their true worth in Christ)

Available Services
　　Travel Consultant (CPPG Travel–Owner)
　　CottonPatch Property Management Service (Owner)
　　Financial Technology Solutions (Wealth Generators–Distributor)

#SOCIALSUICIDE

Tanya E. Lawrence

And they continued stedfastly in the apostles' doctrine and fellowship, and in breaking of bread, and in prayers.
—Acts 2:42 KJV

#Family

Do you remember the times when families would gather for dinner in the evening? I can recall; for this seemed to be the best time of the day. After a long day's work, our family would meet at the dinner table and debrief about the events of our day. Everyone would engage in this time from the youngest to the oldest. Everyone's part was of equal importance.

So much has changed over the years as our lives have been interrupted by the every growing use of social media. There used to be a time where we would meet together to share our views on life, our ideas, attend events to show support for our communities, or even to indulge in the arts for our entertainment sake. It seems these rituals are slowly beginning to lose their savor. In comparison, I think about our meal times now. No longer do we gather to hear the chatter from our day. Our communion time is disturbed by the 'bings' of our email, text, instant message, tweet, or Facebook notifications.

This mountain of entertainment has become a hindrance for many families as we are losing the ability to use our interpersonal skills. Social media has gotten us so distracted from what used to be the simple things in life. Not only does this over usage of social entertainment keep us from being able to have face-to-face interactions, but it can cause one to have increased anxiety and stress. Am I saying that all social media is bad? Of course not. However, if not used with caution, it could be the very thing that could tear your family apart.

I remember enjoying family time with my kids, but now I have to compete for their attention. We are not fighting each other, but fighting against electronic devices that consume so much of our time. At dinner, there is no more conversation, but instead, everyone's face is buried with the flashing lights or scrolling messages of some video game, tablet, or smartphone.

Although, entertainment by way of the World Wide Web makes this mountain hard to climb, there is still hope. To help prevent your family from social suicide you could try the following suggestions.

No Electronic Rule

No electronics at dinner time, school, church, etc. Minimizing use can help cultivate better use of time.

Set a Specific Gathering Time

Make a point to have a designated family night. Play a board game, cards, or create handmade crafts together. Plan a family vacation or getaway to enjoy each other outside of the home.

Have Family Prayer Time

It has been said, "A family that prays together, stays together." It is imperative that you set a time to pray as a family, as this will not only strengthen your family bond, but will also keep God as the centerpiece and covering for your household.

And when the day of Pentecost was fully come, they were all with one accord in one place.

—Acts 2:1 KJV

#Community

Snap, double tap, tweet, like, thumbs up...our lives are now being defined by a series of hashtags and emoji's. We are no longer gathering in one place to be on one accord, but rather the opposite. As we continue to climb the social entertainment mountain, we can see that we now have a variety of options to meet up. There are so many social media forums where people can now connect, communicate, or push their point of view.

I remember when Facebook came on the scene. People used it as an instrument to help high school friends stay connected after graduation. Today, Facebook has evolved into so much more. Social resources now give us the ability to video chat, play games, make purchases, advertise business ideas, and just about anything else we can imagine. People have the tendency to be mass motivated, as we are always looking for ways to stay on top or be knowledgeable of the latest trends. In this day and age, that can be good or bad.

As we continue to climb this mountain, we can see that social media has become the heartbeat that moves and shapes our views of the world. It is what awakens us in our communities. Social media is attributed to the rise of community activism and has drastically affected how we imitate what we feel concerning certain issues. For example, our communities will always remember the imprint that has been made from such movements as #BlackLivesMatter, which spoke to the increase in publicly explicit murders of black citizens by the hands of white police officers. We can recall the massive move of the sports realm after NFL player, Colin Kaepernick 'took a knee' at the singing of the national anthem to denounce and draw attention to the injustices that are happening across the country. We can even see various challenges, such as the ice bucket challenge that was enacted to help bring awareness to the life threatening ALS disease. Whether it is used for good or bad, social media has become the voice that speaks loudest within our communities.

There are many different means for how this medium can be used, but just like most things, there are always pros and cons. The following are just a few, as it relates to the use of social media in our communities.

Pros:
- Social media can be used to reach a mass audience.
- It can be used to encourage, motivate, and teach.
- It can help you stay connected with family and friends.
- You can share ideas, photos, points of interest, etc.
- In business or public relations, you can market, buy, and sell, to people all over the world, who you may not have been able to reach through traditional methods.

Cons:
- Social media can become time consuming, preventing you from focusing on other tasks that should have your attention (e.g., work, family, education, God).
- It can diminish interpersonal skills and limit face-to-face interactions.

- It promotes false realities. People can pose as being someone or something they are not.
- It can create mass hysteria, hatred, exclusions, and discriminatory activity.

We can overcome the social suicide within our community by focusing on the things that are relevant to our personal lives. Don't be so quick to jump on the bandwagon with what everyone else is doing. Know all the facts and not just the ones the media wants you to see. We are living in perilous times and the hearts of many are waxing cold. We are losing our God-given affection for one another. We do not have to fall prey to the corruption of our society, but we can stand as a beacon of hope and inspiration.

Let no corrupt communication proceed out of your mouth, but that which is good to the use of edifying, that it may minister grace unto the hearers.

—Ephesians 4:29 KJV

#SocialAcceptance

Proverbs 18:21 (KJV) tells us, "death and life are in the power of the tongue," but I'm here to tell you that it is also in the power of social media. News from all over the world is being saturated with various attacks and injustices that affect the very fiber of our societies and culture. Too often, we turn on our media sources and hear disheartening stories of individuals, communities, cultures, politics being destroyed by violence and other prejudices.

Groups from all over are diligently working to gain social acceptance in an attempt to win the minds of the masses. We can see the transition of activism that used to be taboo or unheard of, growing in popularity and creating a spiritual downfall from what God created us to be as individuals.

We have seen an increase in crime, violence, and self-hatred because we are allowing ourselves to be defined by how many likes or views we get. We want people to assume we have the best lifestyles, the best personalities, or the best fashionable trends. But what is the real truth behind our character? Who are we really? Are we exemplifying the person that God ordained us to be, or are we emulating a falsehood so that we can please the eyes of a social crowd?

This, by far, may be the most challenging part in this mountain. People are losing their self-worth. People are looking to social media to see what they can obtain versus looking to God – searching within to see the talents that he has already predestined for their lives.

The falsehoods are creating an identity crisis for so many and are allowing deception to reign; ultimately opening a door for us to become a target for inappropriate behavior. Repeatedly, we are seeing young people subjected to many things in an effort to gain social acceptance. Do these sound familiar?

- bullying
- cyber attacks
- identity theft
- scamming
- so-called "haters" (e.g., jealousy, envy)
- defamation of character—just to name a few

It's sad to think that some people get pleasure out of making someone else feel bad. An attempt for social acceptance is becoming the most viral act in committing social suicide.

Not only is it killing hope of one being their true self; but also kills the integrity of what the mediums were originally set to be, which is something good and positive. Again, I'm not saying all social media is bad, but inappropriate and excessive use of it can make it so. To combat this mountain, some general rules to follow should be:

- Don't let other's public opinions define who you are.
- Be happy with the person God created you to be and seek him for the purpose he has for your life.
- Be a good steward of your social resources. Don't participate in negative activity—not only can it hurt someone, but it could also damage your reputation.

Mastering the Mountain
- Don't let social media or excessive entertainment prevent you from balancing your family structure. Trade electronic time for family quality time. No devices!
- Stay relevant in the community, but don't jump on the bandwagon, just because a hashtag marks a massive movement.
- It's okay to be original. You don't have to look for social acceptance. God created you in his own image. Stick to his plan, and prevent social causalities.

Business

Business is a mountain most often disconnected from God. Seldom, if ever, does the world associate God with making money, technological advances, or scientific innovations. As believers, we know the author of it all. More and more discoveries continue to point to the Savior.

Frankly, the best business advice in the world is right in the Bible. As we practice tying the knot between ministry and the marketplace, let's stand strong and tall on this mountain of business.

Gain insight from the following authors:

Tina L. Byrd 149

Malwante R. Stewart 157

Kathy L. Rivers 165

Sarita Price 173

STEPPING AND STANDING
IN THE NAME OF KINGDOM BUSINESS

Tina L. Byrd

Marketplace ministry is a modern day reenactment of God's original creation, God's mandate, and Jesus' great commission to go out and preach the gospel. Jesus did this by spending time in the marketplace, ministering to people in the marketplace, and teaching using business parables.

ABOUT THIS AUTHOR

Tina L. Byrd

With more than 25 years of experience, Tina L. Byrd currently works as a paralegal at one of the top 500 corporate companies in the United States. Having earned a BA from Marquette University and her Paralegal Certificate from Roosevelt University, Tina is serious about both her work and education. Additionally, she is active in her church, serving as Pastor of Administration.

Tina is married, with three adult children and two granddaughters. She loves business-coaching, reading, writing, and traveling. As a business professional, Tina is in the process of launching her own business, 3T Enterprises, LLC, at the 2018 Feed My Soul Women's Retreat which she is hosting in May 2018 in Branson, Missouri.

Connect with this author and speaker for your next event:
Website: *www.3TEnterprisesLLC.com*
Facebook: *Facebook.com/3TEnterprisesLLC/#*
Email: *TinaByrd7@comcast.net*

More from Tina L. Byrd
   GPS Roadmap to Success Planner

Available Services
   Business formation and organization
   Travel consulting

STEPPING AND STANDING
IN THE NAME OF KINGDOM BUSINESS

Tina L. Byrd

Work willingly at whatever you do, as though you were working for the Lord rather than for people.

—Colossians 3:23 NLT

Living Out Marketplace Ministry

The marketplace is a vehicle by which Christians can reflect the image and character of Jesus and convert nonbelievers into disciples. This is easy to see in Matthew 28:19–20.

Living out marketplace ministry became my reality as I
sat in my bathroom one day, with my thoughts and emotions
louder than the running water from the bathtub; I was at the
end of a journey with no direction. I was in the process of losing my house, my marriage was falling apart, my oldest
daughter was acting out, and daily I was battling to stay sane
because I just knew Satan was trying to take my mind. I
prayed, I fasted, I confessed and I stood still, and nothing. As
I sat there contemplating, "What now?" I heard a voice that
said, "You are going to help your pastor teach biblical-based
economics in this region." That voice was louder than the
running water, my thoughts, and my emotions. God had just
spoken to me and I dismissed it. It wasn't until years later
that I realized these three things:

1. My ministry in kingdom business started when
   God spoke to me that day in my bathroom.
2. There are testimonies in tests.

3. There is purpose in pain.

The mandate for the church to conquer and build influence in the area of business and finance is big. So big, that I must first state specifically what my topic will cover as it relates to the mountain of business and finance. I believe there are three main characters in the business/finance mountain: 1) the Christian "employee," 2) the Christian business owner, and 3) the kingdom business owner. My focus will be on the Christian employee; but first I must define all three.

All three characters have confessed Jesus Christ as Lord and Savior and therefore all three should operate at the highest level of service, integrity, and character possible. The Christian business owner and the kingdom business owner, both own their business; whereas, the Christian employee works for someone else. We have more Christian employees than we do Christian business owners or kingdom business owners. The kingdom business owner integrates faith into his or her business' mission statement, services, and resources, including financial resources. Kingdom business owners have a kingdom business mandate, and an extra level of expectation—to glorify God in the marketplace. The Bible says, "Work willingly at whatever you do, as though you were working for the Lord rather than for people" (Colossians 3:23 NLT).

My topic will be limited to the Christian employee and integrating faith in the marketplace. Why? Because there are more believers and nonbelievers in the marketplace than there are Christian business owners and kingdom business owners. I truly believe that the finance side of the mountain of business can be more quickly and efficiently conquered with more Christians as officers of the company, sitting on the Board of Directors and in charge of management, human resources, accounting, legal and marketing. Proverbs 22:29 NLT says, "Do you see any truly competent workers? They will serve kings rather than working for ordinary people." As believers, we must become the voices of counsel and the advisors to those who are in authority. Eventually, this will lead to more Bible-based principles operating in the marketplace, Christian business owners, and eventually more kingdom business owners. That is why it is important that the church becomes proactive in equipping people to serve and glorify God in the marketplace.

There are many Christians in the church who have a heart for God as well as a mind, passion, and giftedness for business; but they are not being equipped to disciple where they work. Christians and nonbelievers work long hours daily side by side, in the marketplace. The marketplace is a venue where we spend most of our hours thus giving us a better opportunity to be a witness and have more impact on others in the workplace. The marketplace is the perfect venue for nonbelievers to see if they really want Jesus to be Lord in their lives.

It's Not a New Thing

The idea of mobilizing Christians for ministry in the business world has existed since the creation of man. The first working business man in the Bible was Adam. God was the author of this discipleship initiative. Adam was discipled by God specifically for work in business. Take a look at Genesis 1:26–28 (NLT), "Then God said, 'Let us make human beings in our image, to be like us. They will reign over the fish in the sea, the birds in the sky, the livestock, all the wild animals on the earth, and the small animals that scurry along the ground.' So God created human beings in his own image. In the image of God he created them; male and female he created them. Then God blessed them and said, 'Be fruitful and multiply. Fill the earth and govern it. Reign over the fish in the sea, the birds in the sky, and all the animals that scurry along the ground.'"

God gave Adam dominion over every living thing. Adam was assigned the job to name all the animals. I would say that Adam was smart and wise. He was senior management. As God's representatives on earth, we must operate in accordance with God's original purpose for us: to have dominion over earth and all that is in it. If business is minimized or removed as a venue to carry out God's purpose, then that will surely and severely undermine the Christian's ability to win souls, spread the gospel and increase God's kingdom.

How Will the Marketplace Mandate Influence the World?

When God put Adam to work, he said, "Be fruitful and increase in number; fill the earth." A business managed by God's people will provide services or products that will help the people in the earth. Our businesses must evangelize, disciple, finance God's kingdom, make profits, produce generational wealth, provide money to others, grow or finance other Christian businesses, and provide help to individuals and institutions that need it.

As Christians are promoted and become prosperous in the marketplace, we must use our wealth to finance and expand God's kingdom. Wealth is a gift from God when made honestly and used in accordance with God's plan. Deuteronomy 8:18 says, "Remember the Lord your God. He is the one who gives you power to be successful, in order to fulfill the covenant he confirmed to your ancestors with an oath." In fact, I believe this is God's will because without finances, especially in this world, God's kingdom cannot be expanded. The money and resources must be available to do God's will and make earth look like heaven.

God's economics have a role in all things and money answers all things. Ecclesiastes 10:19 (NLT) says, "A party gives laughter, wine gives happiness, and money gives everything!"

How Do I Minister in the Marketplace?

Easily. Your actions will speak louder than your verbal "Praise the Lord," and "I am blessed and highly favored." Often, Christians are not invited to vocally share the gospel while at work. Therefore, one's behavior and treatment of people are the best examples of Jesus' image and character on display at work. These nonverbal acts will eventually lead to questions about you and your lifestyle. Sooner or later, coworkers will want your peace, joy, Jesus in their lives too. Even though you haven't said a word, your acts of love, kindness, joy, and faith have. For example, I watched my pastor for years before I finally approached her and said, "I want what you have." What I meant was I wanted her joy, her peace, and her patience. In essence, I was saying, "I want your source," not knowing I was asking for her God. At that time, I was a Christian, with no church home, who had never confessed Jesus Christ as my Lord and Savior. I thought I was good, until I saw a true believer in the workplace.

In summary, Jesus left a huge assignment for us here on earth—go disciple! Since the marketplace is where a majority of our time is spent, it is the perfect venue to evangelize through our Christian character, ethics, and actions.

Mastering the Mountain

- The marketplace is a vehicle by which Christians can reflect the image and character of Jesus and convert nonbelievers into disciples.
- Kingdom business owners have a kingdom business mandate, and an extra level of expectation and that is to glorify God in the marketplace.
- God's economics have a role to play in all things, and money answers all things.

BECOMING FINANCIALLY AWARE

Malwante R. Stewart

Many dream of living what we call the American dream. Although ideas of the American dream may differ from one person to another, for many it is merely wishful thinking. This chapter teaches that when you gain financial knowledge, work in unity, and discover God's plan for your life and begin to walk in your true purpose, your reality can become limitless.

About this Author

Malwante R. Stewart

From a small town in Grenada, Mississippi to the world stage with the United States Army for over 23 years, Malwante Stewart has been giving to our nation and communities. His small-town roots taught him his values and the zeal to always help others and to be giving. He also learned to have fun and enjoy life. As he traveled the world, he did just that—but he also saw that his own community was in trouble. Many in the community needed help with financial understanding.

As a licensed financial professional, Malwante continues to serve the community tirelessly providing one-on-one counseling, budget planning, insurances, retirement funding options, and career opportunities.

Connect with this author and speaker for your next event:
Website: *MSMMissionWorks.com*
Facebook: *LinkedIn.com/in/Malwante-Stewart*
Email: *MSM.MissionWorks@gmail.com*

More from Malwante R. Stewart
    Weekly workshops

Available Services
    Informational/motivational speaking
        (small and large groups)
    Mentoring and Youth Internships
    Military Transitioning Financial Specialist

BECOMING FINANCIALLY AWARE

Malwante R. Stewart

Behold, how good and how pleasant it is for brethren to dwell together in unity! It is like the precious ointment upon the head, that ran down upon the beard, even Aaron's beard: that went down to the skirts of his garments; As the dew of Hermon, and as the dew that descended upon the mountains of Zion: for there the Lord commanded the blessing, even life for evermore.

—Psalm 133 KJV

Having grown up in a small town in Mississippi, I wanted to leave as soon as I could. Like most kids—that little town simply didn't move fast enough for my young mind. We wanted exciting jobs. When one of those super-stores came to town, it was a big deal. The only other jobs were mostly factory positions. But, there were a couple of other options: go to college and get good grades so you can get a good job, but my grades weren't that great in college and with injuries, my track career was over before it got started. My other option was the military.

I was at a crossroad in my life. I had no idea what I wanted to do. As a small boy, my mother, started taking me to the military events that were held by the National Guard. I fell in love with the military, particularly aviation. As a result, while still in high school, I joined the Army National Guard to wear the uniform. I loved the "Be All You Can Be" slogan. It gave me purpose as a young teenager.

As I went into my junior year of college (with bad grades and my first failed relationship), I realized that the military was the best decision I could have ever made. I traveled around the world and back a few times. With the military, I saw how businesses make money and use the government wars to push agendas and expansion of companies. I saw good done in communities that had the right funding to improve. I saw community leaders be great pillars of change when it was thought there was no way. There was only one answer for this, God. He gave me my vision on how and what my future looked like as I was retiring from the army after serving for over 20 years.

God showed me that I would become an educator. This idea was not my first choice or my choice at all. I now know I was meant to touch our community through financial literacy. I was called to teach financial structure. Over the last two years I have had the pleasure of seeing families change because of the knowledge that I shared with them about financial basics.

The lack of economic foundational concepts keeps people from dreaming and living life to the fullest. I believe God wants us to be fruitful and have abundance. Money is referenced in the Bible hundreds of times. Who's actually living this way? We can say it is a disconnect from the church and state, or we can say it is on the individual level that we are disconnected. We all are interconnected in this universe and we have to do our part and fulfill our destiny—God's plan for us. Live your purpose!

We all have to find what our purpose is. I have been led to teach others about money and give a better understanding of this maze as we know it today on the simplest terms I can do.

I have a simple view on business and church. It started at the gathering places for fellowship. Whether on mountaintops, low in the valleys, in small rooms, or mega buildings, ideas are established and supported together. The Word says, "how pleasant it is for brothers to dwell together in unity" (Psalm 133:1 NASB). There isn't one without the other. We as a people have been industrious from the beginning of time, always changing and improving to become the best version of ourselves. Unfortunately, all of this progress can just as easily be used for evil.

Money is often regarded as the evil of society, but the Bible states that the *love* of money is the root of evil. Business owners use money as a tool for leverage, middle class people save and use money for rainy days, and poor people use money to survive to the next day. This is class warfare (as a term from the military) where my business comes into play the most because we are education-based. How do I use my skills as a licensed financial professional to educate our communities?

The reality is that there are too many communities across the country suffering from what is called the generational curse of poverty. As a result of the breakdown in our communities, many are placed in a continuous down turn in the socioeconomic system.

I went through my whole life wanting something that I thought I could never achieve. Like most families today many worry about the day-to-day bills and activities of life (i.e., faith, family, fun, and fitness). Deep down, our goal is to one day live the American dream of owning our own home, some land, and watch our grandchildren grow up. There's nothing wrong with that, but this is not the reality for a large portion of our community. Although life has rudely awakened us from our dreams, there is still hope.

First, we all must have faith in God and allow him to be the beacon that lights our path, because without him nothing is possible. Next thing is to become educated on how business and money works in our society today. To help and give more, we first need to have more. By being in an abundant state with faith on your side, nothing can stop the positive change in our lives. There is no one that I know that doesn't want to do more in their homes, community, jobs, or churches. Knowledge is the key. The people that control wealth are the ones that rule, creating laws, and drafting policies that affect everything we do in life.

What does success look like to you? Should you limit yourself in the journey to achieve it? Are your goals really something you think you can obtain within your lifetime? If we continue to disconnect from each other and from the church, there will be no hope of ever coming back.

The solution, in my eyes, starts at the ground floor within households. We can say that the business owners have all the influence, but I'm not buying that. If we gain financial literacy within all of our communities, it will force a change to happen. We need to know basic principles of banking and budgeting to ensure everyone can be ready if an emergency arises. Today there are roughly 36% of Americans who don't even have $1,000 saved for an unexpected expense or that could be used toward retirement.

If you structure it correctly, money will help you achieve your future goals. I saw this first hand within my own family which gave me the push and purpose for my life. I joined the financial world to teach and spread the word of how you can change your future. I teach how to assign roles for your money, put your money into 'buckets,' and have an accounting system set up within one of your banking accounts as your controls for balance sheets. Get away from just writing notes in your ledger and in the check register. Remove the question out of your hands—use the technology of today. There are many ways to attack this, but I have seen this to be the most direct and seamless approach to having money work for you harder than you work for it. Nevertheless, we have to understand, change isn't just the structuring of our money in the bank as we teach. You have to own something for yourself. Just working forty, fifty, or even sixty years in one place isn't going to give us the ability to live the way we want or give as much as we want.

Finances have a tremendous influence over the family structure. When we finally sit down across the table and look in the eyes of our loves ones, we have to ask a question. Did I do everything in my power to live my purpose? Did I give freely? Did I provide value; and will I be remembered for a life time or a season? I sum that up as how do you lead, protect, and grow the people and the things that you are involved in while you are here. We all must strive to be a positive difference maker.

Mastering the Mountain
- Become self-aware with a purpose.
- Create an opportunity to have something that you own.
- Create a financial structure and life structure that gives you balance and works for you harder than you work for it.

LEGACY—ENCOURAGE DILIGENCE

Kathy L. Rivers

You will leave a legacy. You will be remembered for something—be it good or bad. You will be remembered. Regardless of what we have already done, as long as we have breath in our bodies, there is still time to turn around the harmful things and boost the positive things we have fostered. My heart is to leave a legacy that encourages diligence. I want it said of me that I maintained an upright character. I want my legacy to be that I did not give up—regardless of what anyone else did, or did not do. I lived a life of integrity as a faithpreneur. How do *you* want to be remembered?

ABOUT THIS AUTHOR

Kathy L. Rivers

Kathy Rivers loves to empower, encourage and motivate youths and adults to knowing their identity in God. She is passionate about entrepreneurship and hosts workshops in business. Her deep faith has led her to become a deliverance coach and public speaker on helping others become free from the thoughts of what trauma produces.

She and her husband are currently senior pastors at Kingdom Now Ministries International. She resides in Michigan with her husband Apostle Brian K. Rivers, their 10 children (Kathy's four biological and six bonuses) and 12 grandchildren and counting.

Connect with this author and speaker for your next event:
Instagram: *KRiversApproach*
Facebook: *Facebook.com/RiversYes*
Email: *ApproachKRivers@icloud.com*

More from Kathy L. Rivers
  Remarriage
  From Trau-ma to the True-me (forthcoming)
  Let's Get Started (journal)

Available Services
  Business workshops
  Deliverance coach
  Motivational / inspirational speaker

LEGACY—ENCOURAGE DILIGENCE

Kathy L. Rivers

And if ye have not been faithful in that which is another man's, who shall give you that which is your own?

—Luke 16:12 KJV

Remember the Lord your God. He is the one who gives you power to be successful, in order to fulfill the covenant he confirmed to your ancestors with an oath.

—Deuteronomy 8:18 KJV

Do you see any truly competent workers? They will serve kings rather than working for ordinary people.

—Proverbs22:29 NLT

I took the grandkids to the YMCA (Young Men's Christian Association) this summer. They were so excited to be swimming in the 'big pool,' as they called it. To get in this pool without a life Jacket on, they had to be able to float on their back for a certain amount of time. My grandson, jumping up and down, "Grandma, I can swim, I can swim." I said, "Are you sure, baby? Your mom never told me you could swim." He was insisting that he could do it even though he had taken the test and didn't pass. We decided it was okay and we were going to have fun either way.

That night on the ride home, he was resolute, that the next time he went back, he was going to try again. I encouraged him to try every day until he got it. He owned that idea! He would swim on the living room floor. He would swim in the air all around the house. When it was time for him to take a bath, he would have water all over the floor as he yelled, "Look grandma, I'm swimming!"

We went back to the YMCA two days later. My grandson was so thrilled to be going. As he rushed to get dressed, I tried to calm him by suggesting he slow down a bit. He was having no part of calm. His only response was, "I'm going to pass this time." Sure enough, he did it! He's tenacious about swimming. He didn't let the absence of a pool at home stop him. He practiced without water and continued to speak it and believe he could. His big payoff: he was able to swim and float in the big pool until the very last second before closing. He wanted it badly enough that he would not let anything stop him.

Like my grandson, I have failed and have tried again and again as an entrepreneur. I have been an entrepreneur for nearly three decades. Being an entrepreneur gave me the most flexibility and control over my schedule—particularly as a mother of four. But that's not the reason I became an entrepreneur. I became an entrepreneur as part of my family legacy. I could not get away from being an entrepreneur. It's in my blood from my family and generations before me. God created me for business. This is one of the most passionate topics about which I am always studying to become better.

I have tried corporate America, but clearly it was not for me. As a young mother, I was always looking for that job or career that will be flexible around my four children. Being a semi-single parent in the home, as my spouse in those years, was in out of jail. I simply couldn't make a regular 9-5 job work for me. I had to find babysitters or try to figure out a way to afford daycare from a paycheck that was barely enough to handle the bills. I was that person who called in to the job routinely and would end up close to being fired every other week. My work ethic was great, I learned how to work and work hard at a young age. For years, when I didn't know Christ, we became "street pharmacists" as entrepreneurs. I knew how to sell what I had, put money aside to recoup, and even hired some workers. I called this my default place. I didn't understand the entrepreneur in me. Entrepreneurship on this level became stressful, scary, and taxing on our family. Before I received the Lord's calling, I would cry out to God and think there must be a better way. Growing up with a mother that sold drugs and used drugs, I knew I didn't want that path for my children or myself. Deliverance came and with it came change and freedom from that hustle mentality.

Being an entrepreneur was the legacy handed down through my family. My grandmother was a caterer. People came from miles around to purchase dinners from her. My great grandmother owned a nickel and dime store. She was a successful storeowner right from her home. She sold dinners too. My great grandpa was a farmer. He sold and butchered his meat in the barn behind the house. Although my mother partook in a less honorable business venture as a street pharmacist, she also owned a successful restaurant in Chicago for many years, until I was about 15 years old. Some of my uncles and aunts couldn't read or write because my grandfather took them out of school to work his business in the south. They did not let this stop them. My aunts and uncles also became creative in doing side businesses. The list goes on and on; entrepreneurship is a family blessing.

As I got older and deliverance came to my mind, I began to use my gifts and talents and become what I define as a kingdomprenuer. I became more and more passionate about working for myself. I was a stylist in our kitchen, but it became too stressful on my family and home life. I immediately went into a salon and asked for a job. The owner asked if I had a license and if I knew how to do hair. She decided to let me do someone's hair right in front of her. She hired me on the spot as an apprentice. I got so busy that I began to work in her business as if it was my own business. My booth became my first legitimate business. I learned to work someone else's business with respect and pride as if it was my own. I didn't really know it at the time, but I was following what Jesus said in Luke 16:12 (KJV), "And if ye have not been faithful in that which is another man's, who shall give you that which is your own?"

Even when I moved to a new state, God gave me a strategy on how to build. I cannot say entrepreneurship has been easy. I have done other businesses and declared numerous ideas, but I know in heart that it's God who's doing the increase. "... for it is he who gives you power to get wealth, that he may establish his covenant which he swore to your fathers, as it is this day" (Deuteronomy 8:18 NKJV).

I will say not everyone is called to be an entrepreneur or a kingdompreneur. My purpose of writing this chapter is to help you identify the legacy you are leaving. I also want you to understand that you can't do it on your own—it is God who holds the wisdom and gives the increase. I have discovered over the years that there are many with this talent, or gift, in them that either need to be fined-tuned, know where to start, or simply need someone skilled to help them expand and know how to have integrity and diligence as a kingdompreneur.

The world of technology has made it so easy to get caught in the game and introduce what we have in us to help somebody else as a hustler. I am not against you getting your hustling, meaning work hard to succeed. What is a hustler? The definition I like is the slang version: According to dictionary.com, a person who employs fraudulent or unscrupulous methods to obtain money – swindler. As kingdompreneurs, we are not to do anything at the cost of swindling others to fatten our own wallets. It doesn't surprise me that you see a vast array of entrepreneurs on social media. The world of entrepreneurs has always existed. From the door to door encyclopedia salesman to the 'Madame C. J. Walker.' As kingdompreneurs, we have solutions in us. For example, being in Christ does not mean I have to lower the price of my service for anyone, unless I choose to. I bless people all the time as I feel led. God remains first in my business. I have attended school and seminars to enhance myself in my profession. It is my intent to give you my best at a fair price.

Why do I use the term kingdompreneur. The term 'kingdompreneur' for me is using what I have in me to advance the kingdom of God in my business. It is not a separate entity from me being a businesswoman. God is part of every aspect of my life and it is all for the kingdom. Whether as a man or woman, we are all called to be proficient in our business. This is what the scripture says in the New Living translation, "Do you see any truly competent workers? They will serve kings rather than working for ordinary people" (Proverbs 22:29). It speaks of business ethics. When you see a man (or woman) diligent in business, that man (or woman) will stand before kings.

As kingdompreneurs, we don't have the same business principles as the world does. We are to be diligent, careful, and persistence in our work ethics.

Have Integrity and Character

God will put you before kings. You don't have to be like a crab in the barrel. Do your best and God will reward you. Just as my grandson was determined to swim, you can be that in your business. He didn't let anything hold him back. He set his goal and continued to confess the positive. You do that too. Let it be said that you left a legacy that encouraged diligence.

My Daily Confession

I am a born inventor and entrepreneur. I am no more afraid to step out in faith. I know who and where to put my trust. I can be trusted to carry out the assignment. I will be rewarded. The blessings will live down through my generations. It is fabricated in my DNA!

Mastering the Mountain

- As kingdompreneurs, we don't have the same business principles as the world does. We are to be diligent, careful, and persistence in our work ethics.
- Have integrity and character.
- Work well and God will put you before kings. You don't have to be like a crab in the barrel.

MONEY MANAGEMENT: THE KEY TO HAVING A BETTER RELATIONSHIP WITH YOUR MONEY

Sarita Price

In this chapter on money management, I will share my story on personal finance and introduce five (5) key solutions I use to overcome the money management crisis. These key concepts set me on the trajectory to live a financially worry-free life God's way.

ABOUT THIS AUTHOR

Sarita Price

Sarita Price is an author, board certified life and leadership coach, motivational speaker, licensed and ordained preacher, and a loving and supportive mom who cherishes her daughter. Sarita's vision is to connect present and future leaders through strategic self-awareness coaching, talent development, and empowerment. Sarita is currently the CEO and owner of FSP Enterprise Coaching and Consulting, a business professor at a local college in Memphis, TN as well as an online adjunct business professor for Grand Canyon University in Phoenix AZ. Sarita is board certified through the International Board of Christian Counselors. She is currently attending Grand Canyon University where she is pursuing her Doctorate of Education in Leadership Development.

Connect with this author and speaker for your next event:
Website: *www.FromSaritasPen.com*
Facebook: *Facebook.com/Sarita.Price*
Email: *FSPEnterpriseTN@gmail.com*

More from Sarita Price
   Healing Through & From Sarita's Pen

Available Services
   Life and Leadership coaching
   Inspirational motivational speaking
   Workshops: Work-life Balance / Generational Diversity
   HR Consulting

Money Management: The Key to Having a Better Relationship with Your Money

Sarita Price

The servant to whom he had entrusted the five bags of silver came forward with five more and said, 'Master, you gave me five bags of silver to invest, and I have earned five more.' The master was full of praise. 'Well done, my good and faithful servant. You have been faithful in handling this small amount, so now I will give you many more responsibilities. Let's celebrate together!

—Matthew 25: 20−21 NLT

When most think of the word relationship, the first thing that comes to mind is having a connection or bond with someone or perhaps a romantic relationship. Having a good relationship with your money sounds a little strange to most. Yes, it's a relationship that is very rarely spoken of. Relationships involve many components such as commitment, value, and trust. In addition, when the relationship lacks these factors, it is headed down a path of chaos. This is unhealthy and may cause future issues if not resolved. This can happen with your money as well. Most adults in the United States are living paycheck to paycheck and unfortunately, even more prevalent in certain cultures. Too many people experience more bills than income month after month. We have allowed our money to control us and how we live versus us controlling our money. I have discovered that many households suffer because of this control, or lack of, which often is caused by a poverty mindset and unhealthy societal norms. In this chapter, I will share my personal story about my relationship with money. I will also introduce and discuss five key solutions I used to overcome the money management crisis and set me up to live a financially worry-free life God's way.

My Foundation

I recall as a little girl listening and observing how my parents handled money. My dad was a maintenance worker at a state mental institution in Bolivar, Tennessee. He was also a plumber, and owned and operated his business part time. Routinely I noticed him with his little note pad which he used to track money from both sources of income, as well as listing bills he owed (in which there were very few). My dad did not believe in having a lot of debt. He would always tell me, "Sarita, when you graduate college and start working, always keep six house or rent payments in the bank just in case you become unemployed one day." He instilled in me to put money aside in a savings account for emergencies. I also recalled my dad and mom arguing over money. My mom complained that Dad was tight and cheap. She would always say, "Your daddy will hold a dollar until it hollers," and I would always laugh. My dad was a good provider for his family. He gave me some very good money advice when I was yet a teenager. I remembered all his advice and the advice of others who came across my path as I grew more financial savvy. All this guidance was put into significant use in 2011 when the company I was working for at the time downsized. I had over $6,000 in my savings account before this unforeseen situation happened. Money was tight, yet I could pay my mortgage for more than seven months. I did not lose my home. I re-gained employment and was blessed with a better paying job with better benefits.

Working in the field of finance; having the priceless words of wisdom from my dad; educating myself in the arena of personal finance, and most importantly fighting my own personal financial battles have produced a money manage-ment expert. Next, I will share with you the five (5) key solu-tions that placed me on the path to overcoming money management issues to live a financially worry-free life God's way.

Change Your Mindset

In this chapter's overview, I spoke about the five key so-lutions for having a better relationship with your money. The first key is to change your mindset. It is important to under-stand your attitudes and behaviors regarding money because they drive how you spend your money. For most, the first ex-perience of money management derives from the parents or adults in the home. Culture plays a significant role in how we think about money. Some grew up in homes where genera-tional wealth was the norm. They inherited wealth and were taught principles and concepts to take their inheritance and make more money to leave for their children and grandchil-dren. However, for many other cultures, generational wealth was not present nor a thought. As an African American, I studied my history and observed my community. Genera-tional wealth was never present because of slavery. Once slavery ended, most African Americans were not educated nor did they have the luxury of wealth. When the few started working jobs and gaining skills and knowledge needed to make money, too many had the mindset of 'get money and spend money.' Saving money and leaving an inheritance were not the thoughts of most. My dad was born in 1925, and grew up poor. He was a sharecropper's son, and started off as a sharecropper, but later decided he wanted something better. He was one of the few who had the mindset of saving money and leaving a legacy for his children. A poverty mindset is a generational stronghold in the African-American community that must be diminished. The money that we earn on our jobs or our businesses may not be what we desire. Nevertheless, it is what we do with what we have that matters. Matthew 25:20–23 demonstrates faithful servants being good stewards over that with which God had blessed them. Take what you have and multiply it to leave wealth for your children. In this entire mindset change process, the most important practice that should be first embraced is paying tithes before anything else is paid. Giving God your first fruit (10%) is the most crucial step in the money management process. Tithing will open doors to your success in managing your money and building wealth. This will be discussed in the next section.

Pay Your Tithes, Offering, and Giving

God wants us to prosper spiritually, mentally, physically, and financially. He wants us to break the bondage in our lives so that we can become true stewards for him. He wants us to become free so that we can make an impact for the kingdom. But, you must first give a small part of what he gave us back to him. That's the second key. There are many scriptures in the Bible that speak on tithing. The most well-known scripture is in Malachi.

"Will a man rob God? Yet you have robbed Me! But you say, 'In what way have we robbed You?' In tithes and offerings. You are cursed with a curse, For you have robbed me, even this whole nation. Bring all the tithes into the storehouse, that there may be food in my house, and try me now in this," says the Lord of hosts, "If I will not open for you the windows of heaven and pour out for you such blessing that there will not be room enough to receive it."

—Malachi 3:8–10 NKJV

Not only should you pay your tithes, but also give an offering. Luke says it this way,

"Give, and you will receive. Your gift will return to you in full—pressed down, shaken together to make room for more, running over, and poured into your lap.

—Luke 6:38 NLT

The amount you give will determine the amount you get back." I speak from experience, the more I give, the more it comes back to me—tenfold. Not only does God want us to give, but he also wants us to be knowledgeable about the world in which we live in to truly be productive in the kingdom. We must know and understand how the world operates. You can live in the world without getting caught up in worldly things. This next section talks about educating yourself on financial concepts.

Educate Yourself

There are hundreds and even thousands of books on personal finances. I have read several. There are too many to name in the chapter. Many communities have free financial literacy workshops. As stated earlier, many churches sponsor personal finances workshops and seminars. Some churches, such as the church I attend, have dedicated a ministry to economic empowerment to educate the congregation. Proverbs 18:15 states "Intelligent people are always ready to learn. Their ears are open for knowledge." It is very important to be a sponge and learn all you can. Not only for you, but to give back and help others. One of the first books to start on your financial education journey is the Bible. This is the foundation for all.

Set a Budget

This is the third key and the part of the money management process that many prefer not to discuss and some refuse to follow. However, budgeting is an absolute *must* to experience your financial freedom. Below are just a few tips to follow in budgeting:

- Pay your bills on time (this helps with your credit score and reduces debt).
- Re-evaluate your telephone, cable, and internet needs.
- Take your lunch to work.
- Find a (free) hobby/activity (occupying your time and mind with healthy distractions reduces frivolous spending).
- Shop with cash.
- Make a list and stick to it.
- Eat before you grocery shop and shop alone (whenever possible).
- Beware of sales (only buy what you need).

- Use coupons (but, be careful not to purchase unnecessary items and amounts).
- Consider generic brands and compare products and prices carefully.
- Prepare your own meals (limit your eating out).
- Use what you already have first.

When I started following these tips a few years ago, I saved an average of $200–$400 a month. Utilizing these tips, when I was unemployed, saved money and my peace of mind. It also provided extra money to save and invest, about which we will discuss in the next section.

Save and Invest

In the previous section, I talked about how budgeting helped me to find peace of mind. This peace of mind was due to having extra money to save for what some call a "rainy day." Saving and investing is the fourth key. The rainy day or emergency fund is necessary, because life will bring emergencies (e.g., car repair, household appliances repair, and medical issues). It is always wise to save at least $1,000 for emergencies. Proverbs 21:20 (NLT) states, "The wise have wealth and luxury, but fools spend whatever they get." In other words, wise people save and prepare for the future, but foolish people spend what they get as soon as they get it. Not only is it good to save, but also to invest. Investing your money in stocks, 401k, IRA's, etc. will yield a return on your investment. Check with your financial institution for all the products offered for investing for the future. This is a fantastic way to build wealth to leave a legacy. Deuteronomy 8:18 NLT states, "Remember the Lord your God. He is the one who gives you power to be successful, in order to fulfill the covenant he confirmed to your ancestors with an oath."

The main purpose of this chapter is to educate and empower others financially. Going on the money management journey requires consistency, discipline, and forming good habits. To those who master what I call strategic and productive money management methods, I say go out and become money management disciples. Plan and conduct money management education seminars and workshops. Start an economic empowerment ministry in your church. The first class that my church offered was money management based on biblical principles. That one class was a seed that grew into an economic empowerment ministry. In 2016, I was asked by my pastor to lead the ministry. Not only does the ministry offer money management classes but also other classes for adults in career development, first time homebuyer workshops, entrepreneurship, hospitality, grant writing workshops, and career development for youth. Because of this ministry, many have experienced freedom in their finances as well as their careers. I have personally experienced this freedom. Before I was the leader of our economic empowerment ministry, I was a participant in the yearly conferences as well as a facilitator. I was surrounded by business professionals from whom I learned a great deal. In 2015, God gave me direction to leave my corporate America job after 20 years. I started a coaching and consulting business. The vision God gave me was to connect present and future leadership through strategic life and leadership coaching. I am an advocate of educating and empowering the next generation leaders. The experience from the marketplace combined with ministry has set me on a course of being blessed and being a blessing.

This economic empowerment ministry is producing even more disciples to go out into the marketplace to multiply and have dominion which is one of our main purposes in life.

Mastering the Mountain
- True financial freedom starts with you changing your mindset about money.
- Place God first in your finances.
- Successful money management and wealth building requires consistency, discipline, and forming good habits.

Government

Every person is to be in subjection to the governing authorities. For there is no authority except from God, and those which exist are established by God.

—Romans 13:1 NASB

Regardless of whether the governing body recognizes God as the ultimate authority, it does not negate the fact that he is. Contrary to popular belief, God established this mountain too. It is our job to reclaim it for the kingdom.

Gain insight from the following authors:

Katherine LaVerne Brown 187

Leigh K. Ware 197

Staci L. Kitchen 207

PURSUING A SOUND MIND

Katherine LaVerne Brown

God is declaring order in the land and he has the last say so over everything that affects us. But before there is order in the land, there must be order in our homes and individual lives. We all have the ability as kingdom dwellers to change the climate and atmosphere right where we interact with others on a daily basis. Starting with our own well-being, and extending to members of our households, we will be able to see visible impact on society as a whole.

ABOUT THIS AUTHOR

Katherine LaVerne Brown

As an anointed teacher and ordained elder in the gospel of Jesus Christ, Katherine continues to serve in both prophetic and evangelistic office capacities. One of Katherine's goals is to assist with teaching, training, and equipping of God's people to advance the kingdom of God. Katherine is passionate about educating and training in the various areas within her church, Valley Kingdom Ministries (under the leadership of Apostle H. Daniel Wilson), local communities, various speaking venues, and her missionary work overseas.

Serving in both prophetic and evangelistic capacities, Katherine remains faithful to teaching and training in areas such as prayer, prophecy, evangelism, discipleship, healing and deliverance, and Bible study skills.

Connect with this author and speaker for your next event:
Website: *www.KBrownTeaches.com*
Instagram: *Instagram.com/KathyB1204*
Email: *KBrownTeaches@gmail.com*

More from Katherine LaVerne Brown
   It's Time to Make a Change (complete small group study)
   You, Me, and We Can Succeed (youth activity book set)
   Tying the Knot Between Ministry and the Marketplace (vol. 1), "Hurt to Wholeness"

Available Services
   Motivational Speaker, Teacher, and Workshop Instructor

PURSUING A SOUND MIND

Katherine LaVerne Brown

For we know that all creation has been groaning as in the pains of childbirth right up to the present time. And we believers also groan, even though we have the Holy Spirit within us as a foretaste of future glory, for we long for our bodies to be released from sin and suffering. We, too, wait with eager hope for the day when God will give us our full rights as his adopted children, including the new bodies he has promised us. We were given this hope when we were saved. (If we already have something, we don't need to hope for it. But if we look forward to something we don't yet have, we must wait patiently and confidently.)

—Romans 8:22–25 NLT

As it is written in the book of the words of Isaiah the prophet, saying, The voice of one crying in the wilderness, Prepare ye the way of the Lord, make his paths straight. Every valley shall be filled, and every mountain and hill shall be brought low; and the crooked shall be made straight and the rough ways shall be made smooth; And all flesh shall see the salvation of God.

—Luke 3:1–5 NLT

Our scripture deals with preparing the way for the Lord to bring about salvation within the land. We are preparing the way for the Lord to usher in the Holy Spirit to sweep away the pain and hurt that would cause families to feel they have failed their wounded love ones. Failure causes the entire family to look and wonder what is going to happen to their stability. The family structure is at stake and we all must step up and salvage our lives and point them back into the loving arms of Christ. We can do this, but it is a process.

The Seven Mountains of Influence

These mountains are being challenged and exposed in society today. God's people are on these mountains or sphere of influences and experiencing tumult. It's time to walk in our authority. This chapter will discuss how to pursue a sound mind and bring stability back into your home—dealing with mental illness—the silent killer. One only has to look into their own home, friends, neighbors, or our various communities to see that mental illness is destroying the family structure.

According to *Dictionary.com*, government is defined as the form or system of rule by which a state, community, etc. is governed. A branch of service of the supreme authority of a state or nation, taken as representing the whole. The governing body that sets order and direction in the land, and causes the people to either thrive or perish. In the book of Revelation, it is recorded, "... The kingdoms of this world are become the kingdoms of our Lord, and of his Christ; and he shall reign for ever and ever (Revelation 11:15 KJV). How is this to come about? We as born again believers are on these mountains. We can cause change just by our presence and pursue changing the mindset of individuals we encounter. In the news, there have been great debates about the funding of health care for millions of people in the United States.

There are occasions where we encounter people dying and going without the medication or services that are crucial to the family structure. When we are ill, family support is crucial. Our mind is already trying to:

- analyze why we are ill,
- figure out who is going to take care of us,
- explore the possibilities of whether or not we will come out of this whole, and
- if we will have the money to sustain yourselves.

Recently, several friends of mine spoke about not being able to afford to buy medicine and eat. Some of them had not been to the doctor in years, because there was no money or no health insurance. They were in need and had to choose. I can recall myself, being very ill in 2016. I went to the pharmacy to have my prescription dispensed; I was called back to the counter and informed how much the medicine would cost. I was shocked by the price. "What about my insurance?" I asked. The explanation was that people don't get that prescription filled once they learn the cost. I was too ill to debate. Thank God I had the money, but what about those around me?

Mental Health: The Silent Killer

We will only be discussing one aspect of the health care system—mental Illness. It is destroying families. A silent killer and no one really wants to address it. Mental Illness in various cultures has always been kept hushed and swept under the rug. 'Out of sight, out of mind,' is not facing reality. We must bring it to light as the family structure is being destroyed because no one wants to address the real issue. We need help and its okay to ask for it; pursue and don't stop until someone is listening.

For our discussion, the mental illness disorder refers to a wide range of mental health conditions or disorders that affect the mind, thinking, mood, and the ability to function in social, work or family activities (*www.Psychiatry.org*).

It has been reported that mental illness is more common than cancer, diabetes, or heart disease. More than 26% of all Americans over the age of 18 meet the criteria for having a mental illness. Mental Illness affects not only the person, but the people around them (family). I am not a clinician or a therapist, but I am speaking from personal experiences and looking at our community as a whole.

In the past, mental illness was an issue in some communities or households that was swept under the rug. "Shhhh, don't tell, don't discuss what's happening in the house." I can think back as a child about distant family members being "different." Everyone would say, "Hush child!" or, "Go in the other room!" when that family member was exhibiting behavior that frightened me and brought confusion in the home. Rather than the family seeking out help for the one in need, the family kept the one in need at home and separated from the rest of the family. It is time to expose the root cause of why some households are crumbling. We can get some help to sustain the family or clarity in understanding what is happening that will allow us to become advocates for our loved ones. Remember the Syrophoenician woman in Matthew 15:21–28 who came to Jesus seeking help. Yes, the Lord can heal immediately, but in the meantime, seek out the physical and mental help. Don't be embarrassed. We need to support one another and overcome the fear of exposure with love.

When you speak to individuals, it appears that the family structure is falling apart due to the lack of government funding or healthcare coverage to assist, which is very little and often none at all. What is a person to do? It appears that prisons are overflowing with people that should be in treatment facilities or on medication. Think about some of the homeless people you have encountered. Not all of them are mentally ill, but there are occasions you will speak to someone that appears to have more than a little social distress and lives on the streets with nowhere to go. What is a person to do? We have the answer, as the scriptures says that the earth groans for the children of men to take their place. To us these trials and tribulations are just for a moment in time. However, when the entire household has to suffer in silence, it is for everyone to take a step back and see the broader picture. But there is joy at the end, as in childbirth. We know that we are going to see an end of the tumult.

Recently, I was interviewing some individuals for an assignment, and one of them commented, "There is no place for me to go, but here." This made my heart sad and I ached to embrace this person and say, "It is going to be better." Who will be an advocate for these people; the family had turned their backs because of the mental illness issue.

As a person who has worked at various mental health facilities, over the years, more and more of them have closed and services have become privatized. Privatization is looked upon as a means to deinstitutionalize mental health facilities, cut costs, and save money. But with the controversy over health care coverage overall, treatment is limited for some households if any at all. One only has to turn on the news and see children killing children, incest, rape, murder, drugs and alcohol abuse. What would cause an 11-year-old to plot to kill another 11-year-old? Could this be a form of mental illness or a mental disorder? Often, it stays undetected. That's why we call it a silent killer.

Family Structure Broken

Some years ago, my eldest son, was having issues with one of his daughters. A happy little girl, full of laughter, joy and then something happened. The family was going through a trying time, divorce, and then separation anxiety from their father. After a time, their mother decided to turn full custody over to my son. Sounds good, until my granddaughter started running away from home around age 10. What could have caused this happy little girl to change overnight? Mental illness. This affected the family structure, but how?

The Effects of this Silent Killer

- *workload*: the head of the household may be missing
- *income*: having to spend extra money for counseling or other services
- *schooling*: loss of attendance at school for the ill child and the other children as well
- *behavioral issues*: the other children begin to mimic the behavior thinking this is the way to get attention
- *secrecy*: the unwritten rule comes into play—don't tell what is happening in our household
- *shame*: family members make excuses and live in denial that there is a problem
- *chaos*: loss of sound mind and peace for everyone

My son would go down alleys, looking in dumpsters for his daughter, thinking she must be dead or someone kidnapped her. Why would she keep running away from home? Every time we would hear on the news about a young girl's body found, my son would be on the scene screaming, let me see if that is my daughter. This caused mental anguish for the entire family. This would go on from age 10 to age 18. She would resurface when she was sick or ill. My son would put her in the hospital. There were psychiatric evaluations, but they were limited because of how the guidelines for government funding were structured. He made too much money to qualify for government assistance, but not enough to provide all the care necessary. He made just enough money to get some services, but it was limited. How do you stop treatment for your loved one?

He kept all this secret from me and the world. This is the 21st Century, here we go again. The things I was exposed to as a child are now happening in my immediate family.

I remember coming to his home and he was in tears and said, "Mother help me! I can't get any help from anyone." He thought if my granddaughter came to live with me, things would change. The family was divided. I could only counsel my son to the best of my understanding that pushing or sweeping the problem under the rug would not resolve the issue.

I remember the social worker from a local government agency coming to the home. She was the supervisor and actually said she could not help my son and wanted to know why couldn't I take my granddaughter into my home and raise her. It was hard to contain myself. My granddaughter needed professional care and not to be treated as though there was nothing wrong. I didn't want her to remain a victim of a silent killer. You see, this granddaughter was not only putting her life in danger, but the entire family. Something had to be done.

We kept going from agency to agency, until someone listened. Today, she is still having some struggles, but we know how to deal with her: loving-kindness and recognizing that her struggle with mental illness is real.

If you have experienced this let me give you a few pointers:

- There is money available to help you, but you have to pursue every avenue; and don't give up.
- Keep calling and writing your local government officials and speak up about your community and what is needed. As kingdom dwellers, we walk in favor (Exodus 12:36 and Psalm 5:12).
- In everything give thanks to the Lord and pursue a sound mind for you and everyone in the home. Mental Illness is real. Meditate on 2 Timothy 1:7.
- Yes, by all means pray and seek guidance from the Lord on what to do next.
- Love the individual and love them some more (1 John 3:18 and John 13:34).
- Don't neglect your other children or family members, they need you also (Ephesians 4:2–3).
- Keep telling, shame the devil for he came to kill, steal, and destroy the family structure (John 10:10).
- Speak healing and restoration over your children and family (Deuteronomy 30:3–6).
- Most of all let the power of God shine through you and be an advocate for the kingdom (Isaiah 60:1).
- Remember, you have the ability to change the mindset over this mountain of government.

Mastering the Mountain
- The family structure is important.
- Shame the devil and tell the truth, mental illness is real.
- Love your loved ones and love them some more.

LEAD AND LIVE YOUR LEGACY

Leigh K. Ware

Jails and classrooms taught me about boxes. A box can either confine us or be used to build us. This chapter is significant because it is about something everyone wants; legacy. My life lesson is that you can do more than just leave a legacy, you can also live it. A key point to note here is sight and insight, which exposes the importance of vision on both sides of the coin. Each of us as leaders must be able to see out, but also honest enough to see within. Can we look within ourselves and find the balancing factors for our leadership and developing others coming behind us? Through a review of four principles, I will help you to lead successfully, leverage your influence, and enable you to live your legacy.

ABOUT THIS AUTHOR

Leigh K. Ware

Leigh K. Ware is a consultant, trainer, counselor, and published author. She has firm roots in building the broken, proven through decades of professional success in leadership development and promoting standards, while managing diverse teams within criminal justice, social work, ministry and community initiatives.

It is no wonder that Leigh was awarded the Criminal Justice Command Institute Visionary Leadership Award being that her motto is integrity, parity, and justice. Leigh holds a bachelor's in sociology and a master's in social work. Because of her heart for the things of God and wanting to give him her best, she obtained a doctorate in biblical counseling as well.

Connect with this author and speaker for your next event:
Website: *LeighKWare.com*
Facebook: *Leigh K Ware*
Email: *LKWare@LeighKWare.com*

More from Leigh K. Ware
   Spirit to Spirit
   The Reset Life Journal

Available Services
   Speaking and Training
   Justice Consulting
   Program Development

LEAD AND LIVE YOUR LEGACY

Leigh K. Ware

And He will delight in the fear of the Lord, and He will not judge by what His eyes see, nor make a decision by what His ears hear; but with righteousness He will judge the poor, and decide with fairness for the afflicted of the earth; and He will strike the earth with the rod of His mouth, and with the breath of His lips He will slay the wicked. Also righteousness will be the belt about His loins, and faithfulness the belt about His waist.

—Isaiah 11:3—5 NASB

Introduction

A twenty-year career in law enforcement and social work gave me the opportunity to work with people inside and outside of the walls. Leading programs, working with police departments, counseling people and teaching taught me more than college training ever could. I learned that only my unique voice and fingerprint could bring change. I learned that if I didn't touch it, it wouldn't change, and that every voice matters—that includes yours! Let's unpack this subject together so that you can lead and live your legacy.

Lead and Live Your Legacy: Sight and Insight

The first principle to lead and live your legacy is sight and insight. Excellent leaders are visionaries. Sight is the ability to see the road ahead and work a plan of action to achieve goals that move people from one place to another. Vision is a necessary component of growth and expansion. Mothers and fathers are our first leaders. If they cannot conceive a thought process or mental picture for the family, how can the children be led and the family built? Many lead but they have no sight.

Excellent leaders have insight. Insight is internal and reflective vision. Insight is the ability to see ourselves. We must see not only the problem, but function with compassion, humility, and love. Like Joseph (Bible character in Genesis), leaders face circumstances of turmoil and rejection which produce wisdom and life. In the most difficult times, we do not quit. The result is understanding. How can you quit when you have already seen the promise? The hardest part is seeing yourself and surrendering to the process of the potter's wheel. Insight is critical, and won't be obtained until we take a hard and long look at ourselves: the good, the bad and the ugly and still know that in our imperfection, our purpose is still good. The following are some questions to ask yourself.

- Do you understand what God says about you and how much he cares for you?
- As a leader and a visionary, do you see the big picture of your assignment?
- Do you see the risks and strengths?
- Do you see the solutions to the current and future problems?
- Do you see the strengths of the people to whom you are called?
- Do you see the needs of people assigned to you?
- How has what you have survived in your life connected to your assignment and your greater purpose?
- How does your attitude, mindset, and internal dialog reflect the excellent leadership?

- Have you identified ways to make them better?
- What area of your life needs more humility?
- What area of your life needs more confidence?

Lead and Live Your Legacy: My Small Is Big

Excellent leaders are visionaries and solution carriers. With sight, however comes the burden of what you see. We can observe all that is wrong and how systems fail people. Specifically, in government and education we can see inequity, poverty, unfair practices, lack of access to opportunities, corruption and injustice. We can be overwhelmed and almost depressed by the volume of the problems, and forget that we carry a solution. My grandfather taught me that education is the only thing that no one can take from you. We have the equipment and gifts needed to fix it. Before my swearing in as a Correction Officer in 1994, a family member asked me why I was taking the job. My response was, "If I don't make the system better, who will?"

When you say, "Yes, I am willing to try to do my part, although insignificant," it is then that your small becomes big.

As a counselor, I was asked to create a choir elective program in a women's prison. Of the 82 women in the program, all were receiving treatment for substance abuse. Almost all were mothers, and survivors of trauma, rape, loss, and intimate partner violence. In each session, we learned and a community within a community was formed. The ladies shared hope, joy, and encouragement in the face of despair and darkness. Eventually, they were singing in rooms. I was blessed to watch them find their voice while they uncovered, unveiled and unearthed their purpose in the process. I witnessed them exchange healing for pain, love for loss, and life for grief. Soon we were invited to facilitate events and perform for families and graduations. Together, they learned to face fear courageously. Harmony and recovery happened. I learned that my small is big.

The small things that you create, teach, implement, or change all matter. I encourage and implore you not to run away from what is broken, but run instead to it and build it better. Think about the following questions.

- What have you held in your heart but failed to move forward because you thought it was too small?
- Can you identify small changes that you have already made in your life that have made a big impact for you or others?
- Do you have a dream to start a business, a ministry, an educational program, or other activity that will enable you to serve people?
- Why haven't you started?

Lead and Live Your Legacy: Touch and Be Touched

To lead and live our legacy, we must be willing to touch. We can't be afraid to reach out and make an impact. Excellent leaders have moral courage because they must touch what people don't want changed. Excellent leaders are called to confront and build. How? We touch through creativity which is innovation in action. Excellent leaders are willing to build differently according to the methods they are given which may be opposite current standards and approaches. Excellent leaders are led by the Holy Spirit who is the master builder and architect. When we touch, it means that we bring our thoughts, ideas, solutions, strategies, and commitment to the table of our assignment. We mold the clay. Excellent leaders raise the concept from nothing into something tangible and powerful. They cultivate a project, a system, a program, a protocol, a process, like raising a baby into a full grown man with a mustache! People will say, "You can't touch that!" The response of an excellent leader is, "Yes I can, now watch."

The beautiful thing about touch is that what you touch touches you. Self-care is critical for the life and longevity of the leader. You cannot lead and not be affected by the people and the process. What you build should not just change and improve the system you touched, it should also change you for the better. We should strive to serve with clean hands and a pure heart. Excellent leaders seek to help not cause harm. It is important that we nurture our mind, emotions, body, spirit, and relationships. Self-care will enable us to thrive, not just survive. The following are a few more things to ponder:

- If you are struggling with dirty hands as a leader, what steps can you take to address the condition of your heart, mind, behavior, etc.?
- What barriers are keeping you from taking care of yourself physically, emotionally, spiritually, and relationally?
- If you are experiencing burnout, what steps can you take to revive your heart, hands, and your mind to ensure that you fulfill your purpose and assignment?

Lead and Live Your Legacy: Leave the Door Open

Leave the door open means that you lead with legacy in mind. Leadership is not a solo experience. It ought not be a top dog and everyone else is down structure. Why? Because we limit and restrict ourselves from the beauty, blessing and benefit of people. Instead of top dog, imagine a line across and a two way street.

Legacy is not net worth, properties, or plaques on the wall. Real legacy is not you, it is people. Things can be erased, people cannot. How do you leave the door open and build legacy? By the way you lead, instruct and mentor people and the fingerprint that you leave behind. Government and education are systems. They involve rules, regulations, theories, practices, standards and measures for people, written by people, and carried out by people. You have the ability to change and improve systems by the way you lead, build, and serve. We are always building legacy if we lead with the right heart. Jesus built legacy with his disciples. He was teaching, and living the legacy of his instruction, while he watched them build the kingdom. Legacy is multidimensional and multigenerational.

Team Culture Snapshot

Imagine this team culture snapshot: Our team is a group of people who enrich each other, who help each other, and serve each other. We agree on commonly developed and stated values, mission, and goals. We are people who have accountability to a standard of integrity and to each other.

We should foster a culture of leadership based on the strengths of people, support, thanksgiving, respect, and honor. Great leaders work face to face and heart to heart. This is how you lead and live your legacy.

Conclusion

My eyes saw the possibilities. Justice and integrity could indeed make broken places whole and complete. Then my heart stood before a mirror revealing what was hidden. Truth's fingers reached into those places. Humility rose and met courage to take my itty-bitty, small, and grow it into big. I reached to embrace my assignment, then I realized it was dripping on me bleeding. My prescription for wellness was written and I took the medicine and started walking. Righteousness and the servant's heart danced pioneering a path. Many walked with them together exchanging gifts, freely building. While walking I saw out of the corner of my eye, people laughing and dancing but they had tools in their hands. They had built cities. Yes, they had built cities using the tools of sight and insight.

Mastering the Mountain
- Sight and insight caused my small to be big.
- Touch and be touched.
- Leave the door open.

MAN'S GOVERNMENT, GOD'S JUSTICE: RESTORATION OF HOPE IN A LOST AND BROKEN WORLD

Staci L. Kitchen

My desire is to bring a message of hope to those seeking true justice and wholeness amidst wickedness, suffering, and pain and to point you to the only one who is the restorer of all things. He is the true and living God to whom we have access through our Lord and Savior Jesus Christ.

About this Author

Staci L. Kitchen

Staci L. Kitchen is a woman of God with a passion for justice. She is a marketplace leader with 20 years of experience in mission-driven organizations. Staci is a natural problem solver, servant leader, change agent, full of faith and God's wisdom. She has been an advocate for women, children, and crime victims as well as a prayer warrior and intercessor. Staci has a bachelor's degree in criminology from Ohio State University.

Staci lives in Ohio with her husband Paul, two daughters, two sons, and one daughter-in-law.

Connect with this author and speaker for your next event:
LinkedIn: *LinkedIn.com/in/staci-kitchen-ba778322*
Facebook: *Staci.Kitchen*
Email: *Staci.Lavaughn.Kitchen12@gmail.com*

More from Staci L. Kitchen
  Trainings:
    Strategic Direction and Vision Casting
    Governance
    Leadership Development

Available Services
  Keynote topics: (partial listing)
    leadership, management, decision making, problem solving, Biblical solutions, navigating the marketplace as a believer, business challenges
  Event planning

MAN'S GOVERNMENT, GOD'S JUSTICE: RESTORATION OF HOPE IN A LOST AND BROKEN WORLD

Staci L. Kitchen

Justice and judgment are the habitation of thy throne: mercy and truth shall go before thy face.

—Psalm 189:14 KJV

Everyone is seeking justice. If not for ourselves, then for someone we love or some cause that is near and dear to our hearts. What is justice? Where do we obtain it and who gets it? We are challenged by these questions daily in the face of the ever-present pain, suffering, and oppression of individuals and peoples, and the blatant evil that often accompanies these acts. This leaves humanity with a deep cry for justice that seems to go unheard except in seemingly rare instances where the system works on behalf of the wronged. Other times believers and unbelievers alike are wondering, "Where is God?" While it may appear that God is not intervening in the affairs of mankind, his Word reveals his heart for not just his people, but for the oppressed, the poor and yes, for justice. My desire is to bring a message of hope and to let you know that our search for justice must start with the Savior.

God rules in righteousness. He is not a respecter of persons and neither is his judgment arbitrary. He establishes the standards of justice and he judges all things righteously.

The Old Testament books of the Bible tell how God established laws, ordinances, and principles for his chosen people to live by. In abiding by the first commandment to love him and the second to love our neighbors as ourselves, we would in effect fulfill the whole law. This was the standard of righteousness and justice according to God and the basis of his judgment concerning how we treat others.

Man's Government and System of Justice

The mountain of government represents man's rule. His provision for justice is built into this mountain. Earthly government structures exist to bring order and set standards for living. Citizens expect government to work to administer justice when the standards for order have been violated. It is difficult to obtain true justice in a system that depends on broken men to govern and enforce it. This is evidenced by the existence of a flawed system, which often re-victimizes or further perpetuates injustice. The criminal justice system is just one example, but there are a multitude of instances that not only involve laws, rules and regulations but also practices and conduct that is borne out of the heart of man that perpetuates injustice. This is not God's way.

Man's way of handling wrong cannot achieve God's justice. When injustice or oppression prevails, what we call justice can actually be revenge or punishment. Our judicial system provides a means for individuals to obtain some measure of restoration when their rights or person has been violated. The criminal justice system exists so that those who commit crime may be adjudicated, punished, and deterred from further criminal conduct. The challenge is that laws are not able to change the heart of man, even in our government systems. There continues to be a pattern of injustice stemming from the failure of laws and those charged to enforce them to guard against it. So many are crying out for justice and coming up empty.

Higher Powers

The concept and institution of authority is of God. However, man's systems are of this world. They are able to remain intact because of the authority of God. Therefore, how we address injustices within systems of government by people in authority must be by the wisdom of God. As believers, we must seek God for wisdom on how to respond and submit to his way. Other means may result in short-term changes and the systems may work in our favor sometimes; but true and lasting change requires man turning back to God.

The Cry for Justice

Since I was a little girl, I always had a burden for what was right. I could not have articulated that I had a passion for justice, but I knew I had very pronounced reactions to unrighteousness, people being treated wrongly, cheating, lying, and other forms of violence against people. Such was I before I came to the Lord, but I was one who felt a deep sense of conviction when I felt I had been a party to these sins. I have also had my own testimony of being violated and betrayed by people and systems that I had hoped would protect me and didn't. It leaves deep unhealed wounds that only Jesus can heal. I spent over 10 years working with victims of sexual violence and saw firsthand the struggle to navigate systems and to get them to see people who had been victimized as human; to work through pain and trauma when the systems blamed those who were violated; and watching perpetrators being protected. The fight for justice has its own war wounds that only compound the violation. As an intercessor, I not only experience my own cry for justice but I have come to know the cry of others' as well.

God is clear in his Word that he cares about the widows, the fatherless, the poor, and how we are to treat the sojourner or stranger.

Finding Hope

I have much respect for government. As much as we disagree with man-made systems of government, God honors the authority that has been established in our government structures. Many have been called to be a light in the various mountains to bring the kingdom of God to bear. Let's examine some areas in which believers can impact this mountain of government.

Acknowledge God—We need God, our nation needs God, mankind needs God. We must seek to know his will and purpose for humanity.

Pray for those in authority in government—Regardless of how we feel about those in authority and those charged with the systems in government, we must cry out to God for his justice to prevail. The heart of the king is in his hand.

Deal righteously and honestly—For those who are positioned as leaders, lawmakers, law enforcers, judiciary etc., carry out your role as a godly leader.

Be a light—Demonstrate the love of Christ on the mountain of government. Speak the truth in love, speak boldly against injustice. Silence is interpreted as agreement. Actively participate in developing laws and rules that foster justice and righteousness.

Forgive and repent—God says that if we don't forgive those who have trespassed against us then he won't forgive us. By our example of forgiveness, we teach others to forgive as well.

Trust in God—Government is established to bring order. We need government. However, man is fallible. We put so much confidence in man and man-made systems to fulfill our need for justice, to make us whole. Only God can restore and make one whole when loss is suffered. The systems of this world may restore some things, but only God can heal a person totally. We must keep our eye on the Savior and not place our hope in man.

Don't take matters into your own hands—We often want revenge or payback, we want people and the wicked systems to pay for their wrong and we want to make them suffer. God says he will repay. Yes, we can trust God to deal according to his righteousness.

I have my own testimony of trusting God in the midst of being let down by man's system. A person at a bank forged my name on a document that bound me to an organization's debt once the organization folded. The organization folded under my leadership. It was a very difficult season of my life. The bank sued me and obtained a judgment against me and garnished my wages for almost 3 years and then once the debt was paid, they came after me for the interest. It was a demonic judgment from the pits of hell. I had come to terms with all the mistakes I made in positioning myself out of God's will and I repented and had returned to the Lord after having fallen away for almost 10 years. Once I found out that my name had been forged, I sought an attorney and paid an expert witness who was able to verify that the signature was not mine. The statute of limitations on my type of case was 1 year. The only exception was in cases of fraud. Though I discovered the fraud years later, I filed my case, believing I surely would win. I had turned my life over to the Lord; and had surrendered, and begun to seek his will for my life. Not to mention, I had an attorney, expert witness and the law on my side—or so I thought. The case took almost a year and I just waited patiently. Just knowing that somehow, I would be vindicated and all that was unjustly taken would be restored. I remember receiving the call from my attorney that the bank asked for a summary judgment on the basis of the statute of limitations. I was not there to plead my case so I expected that my attorney would do so. Whatever happened in that courtroom, the point was I had lost. I was at a training in the convention center and I just remember sucking back the tears and saying, "God, this is about my faith." I did not care about the money any longer I just needed to know that surely God would not leave me having known that a miscarriage of justice had been perpetrated against me and the one who did it got away with it—with the help of the system. I found a seat to eat my lunch and a man saw me pray over my food. He re-marked, "you don't see that often anymore." I forced a smile but inside I was broken and didn't understand. But I made a decision to continue trusting God. Some believe the system is broken. But, we must not lose sight of the fact that, the system is of this world, so it works as it was fashioned to work. We are in the world but not of the world and no matter what happens, we have to know God is for us. If people in the system allow the injustices, then they will continue. When we step out of God's will through sin and disobedience then we will surely fall prey to injustice. If we fail to do justice when it is in our power to do so, then we perpetuate injustice and uphold the systems that do likewise.

Conclusion

We must renew our minds and our thinking with God's perspective of justice and align our hearts accordingly. In do-ing so, we will be carriers of God's justice and will see change in government. This will require us to put away our carnal responses to injustice and do the Word—this must happen in the halls of justice, the boardrooms, in the town halls, and every place where people of God have been set in authority. The systems don't change themselves, they require people like you and me who have a passion for justice and God's heart for the weak and oppressed to lead change.

Mastering the Mountain

- God has a standard of justice and those who suffer in-justice are near to his heart.

- Man-made systems of government are limited in their ability to protect and restore those who are vulnerable to oppression and often foster injustice.
- Man must return to God and advance the cause of justice and judgment in our government systems.

AFTERWORD

Dear Faithpreneur,

As believers, we have been called to stand firm on each mountain. This book is filled with unique perspectives on how to do just that. It is bursting with insights as to how the seven cultural mountains affect us and how we are to respond.

I hope you have not simply read through this book, but meditated, prayed, and sought God as to what he would have you to do.

It is the deepest desire of my heart that you be nourished by this project. I pray that your eyes are opened to new ideas and thinking. Most of all, I pray you develop a closer walk with our Savior and become excellent in your endeavors as you continue to tie the knot between ministry and the marketplace.

Reclaiming the mountains for the kingdom,

Coach Debora
Taylor-Made International Institute

MEET DEBORA D. TAYLOR

Debora Taylor is the founder and president of Taylor-Made International Institute and its para-church, the Faith and Business Ministry, which produced its first book series aptly titled: *Tying the Knot Between Ministry and the Marketplace*. She received her formal education from the Milwaukee Theological Institute and the Springfield College with a bachelor's in human services.

She was raised in the inner city in the West Lawn housing project. Although she was an atheist for most of her teen and young adult years, at the age of twenty-six, God touched her life. Through the supernatural power of the Holy Spirit, she made her confession for the Lord Jesus Christ. Her life was changed that day, and she has never been the same.

Debora has been a spiritual and integral leader in the human service field for more than twenty-five years with expertise in the areas of women's issues, marriage and family enrichment, youth and early childhood, and responsible fatherhood. Her efforts, her enthusiasm, and her great successes continue to be recognized locally and nationally. Debora has a long list of honors and awards including, the National Presidential Volunteer Service Award for 2012 presented to her by President Barack Obama for her local, regional and national involvement through the United States.

By the leading of the Holy Spirit, Debora and her husband became organizers and church planters of the New Life Kingdom Ministries International. She co-pastored for 18 years with her husband, Pastor Guy Taylor, until retiring from pulpit ministry in 2013 to move south to Memphis, Tennessee. She has been an ordained minister for twenty-eight years.

Debora, fondly known as "Pastor D," serves in ministry partnership with Apostle Ricky D. Floyd and Pastor Shelia Floyd of Pursuit of God Transformation Center International in Memphis, Tennessee.

Debora Taylor, a native of Milwaukee, Wisconsin, now resides in Collierville, Tennessee with her husband. They have two adult children: Nyshi Taylor-Williams and Dominique Taylor. The loves of her life are her granddaughters: My'Asha and Gracelyn.

Debora D. Taylor—International Best-Selling Author
Publications:
> *The Faithpreneur's Handbook: Foundational Wisdom Through Practical Applications*

> *The Faithpreneur's Workbook*

Co-authored projects:
> *Tying the Knot Between Ministry and the Marketplace Volume 1*
> Compiler: Deborah D. Taylor

> *Bruised But Not Broken*
> Compiler: Linda Ellis Eastman

> *Boys to Men: The Guide for African American Boys*
> Compiler: Linda Ellis Eastman

> *Empowered Women of Social Media Volume 1*
> Compiler: Carla Hall and Denise Thompson

> *Empowered Women of Social Media: Finding Global Unity*
> Compiler: Carla Hall and Denise Thompson

Chocolate & Diamonds for the Woman's Soul
Celebrating the Majesty of Motherhood
Compiler: Hot Pink Publishing

Connect with Debora D. Taylor for your next event:
Website: *www.DeboraDTaylor.com*
Facebook: *Faith and Business:*
    Tying the Knot Between Ministry and the Marketplace
Email: *DeboraDTaylor@DeboraDTaylor.com*
Mail: Taylor-Made International Institute
                P.O. Box 1554 * Collierville, TN 38027

———————

Debora D. Taylor
Taylor-Made International Institute

Made in the USA
Lexington, KY
01 June 2018